VALLE GRANDE

VALLE GRANDE

A HISTORY OF THE
BACA LOCATION NO. 1

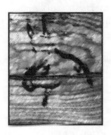

CRAIG MARTIN

Published by
All Seasons Publishing
465 Grand Canyon Drive
Los Alamos, New Mexico 87544

ISBN 0-9639040-4-3

To the memory of my father, Harry Martin

CONTENTS

PREFACE

In July 2001 the Valles Caldera National Preserve Board of
Trustees began planning the first public tours of the Preserve.
The board asked if I would organize volunteers to act as guides for
a short walking tour of the headquarters area. It was no problem
finding 150 eager people who had always wanted to visit the Baca
Ranch, as it had been called for the previous 37 years. In Los
Alamos, Jemez Pueblo, Santa Fe, and Albuquerque, I found plenty
of skilled guides to serve as teachers to the 1,500 or so lucky
people who filled nine bus loads a day for six days. I recruited
experts on the local landscape to prepare the guides for their
task. We all learned about volcanoes, pre-history, ecology, and
changes to the landscape. But when we took our tour groups out,
the majority of the questions from the visitors were about the
history of the ranch. We had only uncertain answers to the
inquiries about how a nearly 100,000-acre parcel of valuable
grazing land had remained intact and available to become part of
the national forest system. By the end of the first tour, I was
kicking around the idea that I would write a book on the history of
the property.

To be honest, when the Baca Ranch came up for sale in 1999 I didn't care whether or not it became public land. Six hectic days of overseeing the tours didn't change my mind. However, a couple of weeks later the trustees asked me to investigate easy hiking routes for future tours. I spent a week walking old roads and trails within the once-forbidden property. Poking into the canyons and hillsides of the Preserve, I was hooked on the attractions of the landscape and on writing about the history of the Baca Ranch.

During my week of exploration, I learned the secret of the Preserve. It has nothing to do with wilderness or a pristine landscape—indeed, the Baca Ranch is one of the most extensively used properties I've ever seen. The Preserve's most valuable commodity is its sense of space. The rest of world seems so very far away from within the vast bowl of the Valle Grande or from the top of the encircling mountains. Without a confining forest to block the view, within the grasslands I could sense an almost-palpable cushion between myself and the world beyond the valley. I knew that each day there were no more than a dozen people sharing with me the 88,000 acres of the Preserve. I almost had the place to myself. It is my fervent wish that every visitor to the Preserve can experience that same feeling of space.

In this book I have tried to lay out a simple history of the Baca Location No. 1, with an emphasis on the human element, starting with the arrival of the Spanish settlers along the Rio Grande. I have included a rough sketch of the geologic history of the Valles Caldera not only because it is of great interest but because the rugged volcanic landscape acted to isolate the central Jemez Mountains. This in turn created a unique history that is set apart from that of the rest of northern New Mexico. In addition, the formation of the Valles Caldera created the extensive grasslands that drew the first private owners of the property to select it from the public domain as compensation for a land dispute. Grass and solitude, both the direct result of the colossal eruptions of the Jemez volcano, influenced the human use of the landscape.

Over the years stories about the Baca Location based on speculation and rumor have been told and retold. Many proved to disintegrate under close scrutiny. For that reason I have used original sources to reconstruct as much of the history as possible. However, there are notable gaps in the available record: the Cabeza de Baca family members, scattered across northern New Mexico, left few details of their ownership; the records of John Watts, would prove enlightening for this story; and the where-abouts of the Otero family records, if any exist, are unknown.

As much as I love ferreting out the details of a story in musty old documents, this book relied on personal contributions from many scholars who have invested years in investigating specific aspects of the story of the Jemez Mountains. Each deserves my thanks for steering me down the right roads in my research. Craig Allen, landscape ecologist at the Jemez Mountain Field Station, provided an overview of the region that encompassed many aspects of the complete history and shared materials collected during his twenty years of research in the Jemez. For geology I turned to many local scientists who have devoted years unraveling the complex tale hidden in the pile of volcanic rock in and around the caldera: discussions with Grant Heiken and Steve Reneau elevated my understanding of the geology from a cluster of misconceptions to a firm base in reality. Ana Steffen introduced me to a variety of archeological sites, granted permission to use photos, and provided a basic knowledge of the prehistory of the Preserve and of the importance of obsidian to that history. Fraser Goff and Jamie Gardner provided details of the geothermal projects on the Baca spiced with amusing personal accounts about those heady days.

Dorothy Hoard, a friend who shares the passion for pursuing a sense of place, doggedly hunted down many of the details about cabins and roads, and was a frequent companion on field investigations. Dorothy always kept me from making unjustifiable leaps of faith, directed my eye to details, and has helped make this a more complete work. Her careful review of the manuscript made the book more clear and accurate. A detailed edit of the manuscript by Rebecca Shankland corrected my perpetual misuse of commas and participles and helped clarify numerous sections. I owe Becky a huge debt. My wife, June Fabryka-Martin, turned her skilled eye for detail to these pages and ferreted out many errors. Colleague and friend John Hogan was of great assistance in tracking down photos and in helping establish my sense of place.

With good cheer and kind words, Rebecca Collinsworth and Marianne Mortenson at the Los Alamos Historical Society Archives bore the brunt of my impatience to follow up on a new lead during my unannounced arrivals at their office. The patient staff at the New Mexico State Record Center and Archives pointed me in the right direction on numerous occasions. Volume after volume of deed records were provided by the Sandoval County Clerk's office. After a month of futile searching, an e-mail to the Supreme Court Library yielded the record of the opinion of the Eighth Circuit Court on the United States vs. Redondo Development Company, thanks to work of Carroll Hawley. John Sparks permitted me the use of his diary of the Sparks brothers' journey through New Mexico. William DeBuys—cultural historian and the first chairman of the Valles Caldera Board of Trustees—shared his hard work on the journal of Vernon Bailey, and his exquisite sense of balance served as an inspiration on many levels. Kurt Anschuetz and Thomas Merlan provided their draft annotated bibliography of the land-use history of the Baca Location and brought

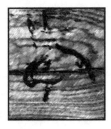

Brand of the Baca Land and Cattle Company

several important documents to my attention. Tom's dogged search yielded among other things the court records related to the Whitney partition suit, which are an immense contribution to the documented history of the Baca Location No. 1.

Gary Ziehe, Executive Director of the Valles Caldera Trust, shared his inside knowledge of the development of the legislation that created the Preserve and encouraged this work from the beginning. Gary, Ranch Manager Dennis Trujillo, and the entire Trust staff permitted access to the ranch to allow me to paint a more accurate portrait of the property. Another trustee, David Yepa, guided me on finding details of legal matters and enriched my understanding of the relationship betweem Jemez Pueblo and the caldera. Joel Roth provided copies of the photographs of Robert Baxter taken on the ground during the logging operations in the late 1960s. Vernon Glover searched dusty old files to dig out information on the New Mexico Timber Company on the Baca Location.

Others took time for interviews that provided details that led to new discoveries: Dan and MaryAnn Bunten on the Bond family's love of the Valle Grande; Linda and Jim Goforth on the stories of George White; former Governor Bruce King on the King brothers' days on the Baca Ranch; Randy McKee on cattle ranching; Bill Huey on Pat Dunigan's relationship to the land; and Andrew Dunigan on his family's ownership of the property. To all of the above, my sincere thanks.

Because of its unique management directives, the Valles Caldera National Preserve is unlike any other public unit of the federal land management system. It is not managed by a federal employee, but by a board of public trustees. Congress specifically laid out the ground rules to facilitate experimenting with new ideas, to minimize the management bureaucracy, and to allow a different type of outdoor recreation, all while protecting the essential nature of the landscape. I've touched on the current management challenges facing the Preserve in Chapter 11, but I leave it to a future author to set down the history of the Preserve under public ownership. It will undoubtedly rival the intricacies of the tale up to 2000.

Because I'm a fisherman, hiker, and backpacker, cows aren't high on my list of favorite mammals. Cows trample precious undercut banks where trout should grow as long as your forearm. Their pie-sized ploppings can make a meadow smell like a waste-water treatment plant. They can help transform pastures of native grasses into a hodge-podge of vegetation species that have no business growing in New Mexico. But after a year of digging into the story of the Baca Location No. 1, cattle seem a natural part of the landscape of the Preserve. Since at least 1835, Hispanic and later Anglo stockmen have brought their herds to *Los Valles* for the summer. Descriptions of the valleys by visitors ranging from Adolph Bandelier to Bruce King include references to grazing animals. The prospect of grazing sheep and cattle is what brought most of the property's owners to invest in the land and make it their home for at least part of the year.

Like everyone else, I have my opinions about how the Preserve should be managed. Despite the tradition of grazing, I would love to see cattle excluded from the back valleys—the San Antonio, the Toledo, and the Valle de los Posos—but if the ranch must be a working one, then a well-managed, carefully monitored herd in the Valle Grande provides an accurate portrait of the property's history. For this piece of property, it just might be the right thing.

During the summer of 2002, I presented a summary of the information in this book on guided hikes on the Preserve. Few of us like to hike with a guide, but it is likely that not many recreational pursuits on the Preserve will be organized along standard lines. As a guide I felt somewhat like an intruder on each hiker's sense of space, but most of the participants expressed appreciation of my lecture-on-the-hoof. Like the grazing cows, the presence of a guide was a reach toward the center. With Preserve management a blank slate, thousands of people with dozens of points of view will show up with chalk in hand, ready to scribble recommendations about their own special interest. The only way to manage the Valles Caldera National Preserve is to approach that center balance where no one may be completely satisfied, but at least most are willing to live with the compromise.

For me, researching this book has been a journey toward the center through an understanding of the landscape. Given the difficult assignment of the Valles Caldera Trust to run a working ranch that provides access to the public, I hope these pages help move the reader away from the extremes and toward an understanding of a balance of management policies.

Los Alamos, New Mexico
July 2003

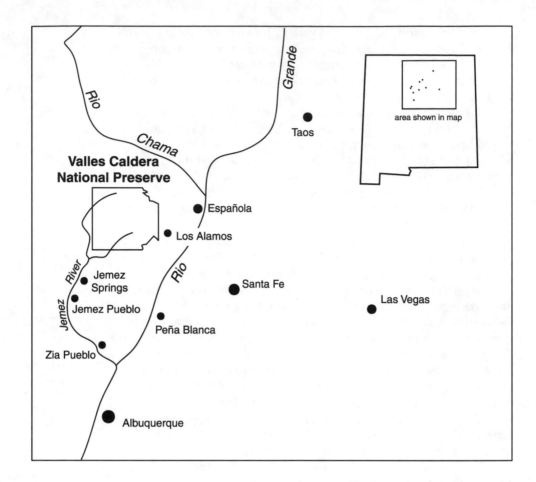

The location of the
Valles Caldera
National Preserve
in northern New
Mexico.

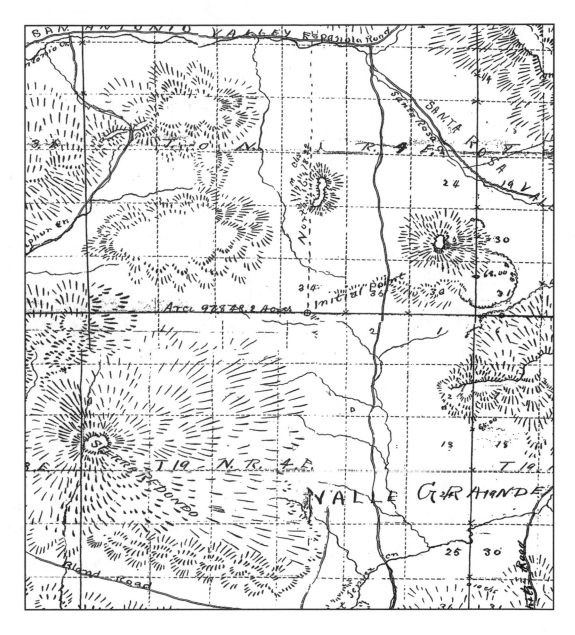

Sketch map of the Baca Location No. 1 drawn by U. S. Deputy Surveyor Walter G. Marmon, about 1898.

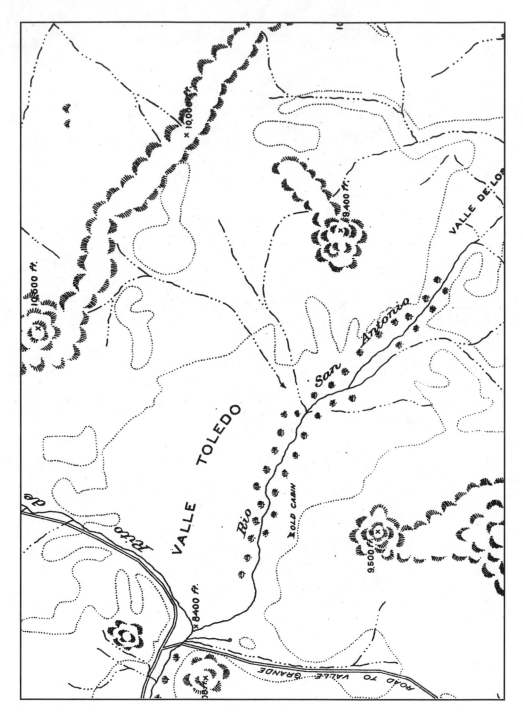

*Part of sketch map of
the Baca Location No. 1
drawn by L. D. W.
Shelton for the Redondo
Development Company,
1909.*

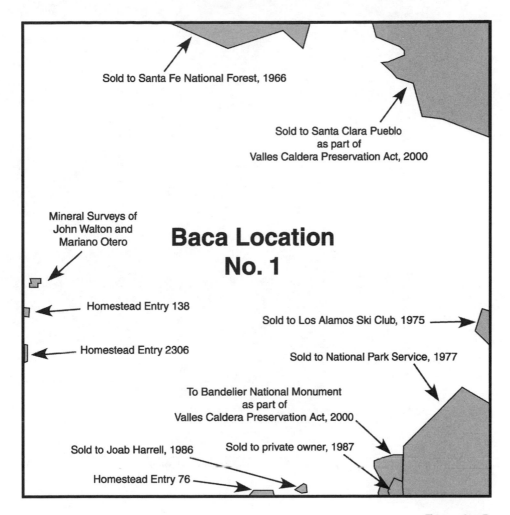

Sold to Santa Fe National Forest, 1966

Sold to Santa Clara Pueblo
as part of
Valles Caldera Preservation Act, 2000

Mineral Surveys of
John Walton and
Mariano Otero

Baca Location
No. 1

Homestead Entry 138

Sold to Los Alamos Ski Club, 1975

Homestead Entry 2306

Sold to National Park Service, 1977

To Bandelier National Monument
as part of
Valles Caldera Preservation Act, 2000

Sold to Joab Harrell, 1986

Sold to private owner, 1987

Homestead Entry 76

From the Baca Location No. 1 to the Valles Caldera National Preserve. Since the original square boundary line was drawn in 1876, the outline of the property changed many times. The Baca Location No. 1 encompassed 99,289.39 acres; the Valles Caldera National Preserve holds about 89,000 acres. Based on a map in the 1993 study of the Baca Location No. 1 by the Santa Fe National Forest.

CHAPTER ONE

BIG BANGS:
THE VOLCANIC HISTORY OF THE
VALLES CALDERA

The human history of the Valles Caldera is but a thin blanket draped over the contours of the landscape, taking its shape from the mountains, rents, moats, and yawning craters below. Forces on a planetary scale, driven by the currents emanating from the earth's mantle, shaped the Jemez Mountains and created a circular fortress that protected the resources of the mountains from invasions by those who lived on the frontier until well into the twentieth century.

In simplest terms, the Jemez Mountains are a massive pile of a variety of lava types sitting atop an immense geologic X formed by two fundamental cracks in the crust of the earth. An impressive pit—the Valles Caldera—lies at the middle of the volcanic pile.

Slicing New Mexico roughly in half from north to south is the Rio Grande rift. Like its younger, more easily understood counterpart in Africa, the rift is a surface expression of tectonic forces

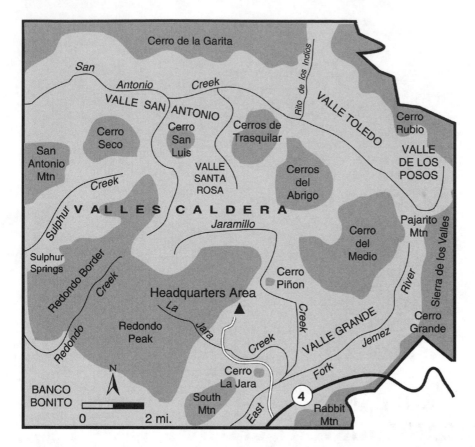

Map labels:
Cerro de la Garita
Rito de los Indios
San Antonio Creek
VALLE SAN ANTONIO
VALLE TOLEDO
Cerro Rubio
Cerro Seco
Cerro San Luis
Cerros de Trasquilar
San Antonio Mtn
VALLE DE LOS POSOS
Creek
VALLE SANTA ROSA
Cerros del Abrigo
VALLES CALDERA
Sulphur
Jaramillo
Cerro del Medio
Pajarito Mtn
Sierra de los Valles
Sulphur Springs
Redondo Border
Creek
Cerro Piñon
Headquarters Area
La Jara
River
Redondo
Redondo Peak
Creek
VALLE GRANDE
Jemez
Cerro Grande
N
Cerro La Jara
Fork
BANCO BONITO
South Mtn
East
4
Rabbit Mtn
0   2 mi.

Modern place names of the major features in the Valles Caldera National Preserve.

that are pulling apart the earth's crust beneath the state. This stretching thins the crust and shatters it with deep cracks. The thinning of the crust permits large bodies of magma to rise to less than 20 miles from the surface. In addition, faults can be a conduit for magma from these shallow magma bodies to the surface. The Rio Grande rift is a zone of abundant volcanic activity.

But the monstrous pile of the Jemez Mountains has an even more complex genesis. A second weakness in the earth's crust, the Jemez lineament, runs southwest to northeast across the Southwest from Arizona to southern Colorado. Expressed on the surface as a band of volcanoes, one can easily trace the lineament on a map by following the splotchy black of lava flows from the White Mountains of Arizona through the Taos area and to the north. Within the Jemez range, the line follows Cañon de San Diego and Redondo Creek. The lineament is probably located on an ancient fault in the Precambrian basement rocks far below the surface. Indeed, the rocks on either side of the lineament are different in age and suggest that the fault may be a suture of two small continents from the distant past.

The Jemez Mountain volcanic field straddles the intersection of these two immense gashes in the earth's crust, and that junction provides a pathway for staggering amounts of molten rock to flow to the surface.

About 16 million years ago, the first mantle-derived magma in the Jemez region flowed onto the surface along the boundary of the Rio Grande rift. These basalts—hot, flowing lava typified by Hawaiian volcanoes—were an innocent beginning to the lava mound. After a three-million-year quiet period, mound building began in earnest. More viscous lavas formed domes; other hot rocks flowed east into the Rio Grande rift. Volcanic activity intensified between ten and seven million years ago with the eruption of the viscous lava andesite from numerous vents. More than 225 cubic miles of rock—about half the volume of the entire Jemez range—erupted over the course of three million years. The lumpy mound was starting to look like a mountain.[1]

As if exhausted by this massive outpouring of lava, around seven million years ago flow volumes from the Jemez volcanic field were greatly reduced. However, some volcanic activity continued and over the next three million years focused on the northeastern quarter of the volcanic field. Flows had occurred in this area since the beginning of activity in the volcanic field, but during this later time period tall domes formed along the eastern edge of the field. Composed mainly of the extremely viscous dacite, these mounds formed the mountains of the Sierra de los Valles and the familiar backdrop to Los Alamos of Cerro Grande, Pajarito Mountain, Caballo Mountain, and Tschicoma Peak.

What was the profile of the Jemez Mountains four million years ago? The classic image of the symmetrical cone of a Cascade Mountains stratovolcano doesn't apply to the early Jemez range. It did not look like Mounts Rainier or Hood, despite persistent misconceptions to the contrary. Given widely spread eruption centers and the ten million years of volcanic activity in the area, the range was a complex feature of fresh lava domes, eroded old cones, and deeply incised canyons. Rather than pointing skyward with a single peak, the Jemez region was a collection of lesser peaks much as it is today. The summit of the range probably never surpassed its present pinnacle of 11,254 feet.

About 1.75 million years ago, at least two explosions rocked the southwestern portion of the mountains. Spewing towering plumes, two small volcanic vents signaled the beginning of a new, far more violent type of eruption. Highly viscous, gas-filled magma held together until building pressure literally blew the rock into fine fragments. Frothy with expanding gases, the lava was nothing more than ash and cinder and bombs of pumice. Below the surface, the sudden release of pressure above shot great quantities of rock through the vent like champagne from the neck of an uncorked bottle. Suddenly, the ground surface above the magma

"The imagination staggers at the violence and turmoil of this material as it surged through the gaps in the surrounding peaks and cubic miles of it spread over hundreds of square miles of country, filling canyons…"

Clarence S. Ross, writing for New Mexico Magazine, *January 1962.*

Schematic of caldera formation. (a) A rising magma chamber domes and fractures the overlying rocks.
(b) Magma finds the zones of weakness and explodes from a ring of fractures.
(c) So much magma erupts from the chamber that the roof collapses.
(d) The basin left by the collapse fills with sediment and small domes form along the ring fractures.

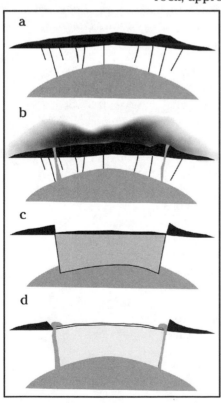

chamber was unsupported and collapsed into the void. Two small collapse craters—called calderas—sat within the volcanic field.

But after 14 million years of lava movement, the dramatic volcanic activity in the Jemez Mountains had barely begun.

The composition of the magma in the chamber beneath the surface determines the patterns of eruption of a volcano. Beneath the Jemez volcanic field, a pod of molten rock had been pushing toward the surface since the activity began. By 1.6 million years ago the magma was rich in silica, which creates a sticky, viscous material. Deep within the earth, extreme pressure from the mass of the overlying rock keeps gases and steam in solution. When such material approaches the surface it does not flow as rivers of molten rock but forms bulges and domes that seem to grow from the inside. This type of eruptive sequence creates steep-sided cones.

The magma is also characterized by its ability to trap expanding gases, which builds internal strain to a high break point when a sudden release of pressure fractures the magma into fragments called pyroclasts. Tiny pyroclasts are called ash; pebble to fist-sized pyroclasts frothed by escaping gases often form pumice; larger pyroclasts can form volcanic bombs..

Such a magma pod, rising buoyantly through cooler, denser rock, approached the surface in the Jemez range around 1.6 million years ago. The surface above began to rise slowly to form a low dome. To relieve some of the tension, circular faults formed in the crust. The stage was set for a colossal event.

From a vantage point more than a million years in the future, it is impossible to tell the type of day it was when the Jemez volcanic field began its transformation. However, by reading tiny details of the rock record and applying observations from modern-day volcanoes, geologists have pieced together parts of the story. Volcanic eruptions are often announced by a series of small earthquakes. So it is likely that over a period of weeks or months, the Jemez rumbled from within as magma worked up through the circular fault system. Finally, one of the movements permitted magma to enter a zone of weakness where the overlying material could no longer contain the pressures in the magma below. In a matter of seconds, the escaping gases fragmented the rock and blew a hole through the surface. A towering plume of hot rock and gases burst straight up from the fault. The column reached a height of about 60,000 feet, propelled by the rapid release and expansion of gases from the vent. Strong winds blew the frothy rock pieces—pumice—to the east where they rained down on the landscape. Pumice was deposited in beds up to 30 feet thick more than 15 miles from the vent; the beds are thickest in the west and thinnest to the east.

The initial explosive phase of the eruption emitted a constant, enormous stream of ash and gas. Material at the top of the magma chamber was being erupted faster than deeper magma could flow in and fill the void. The top of the magma body was expended, and with

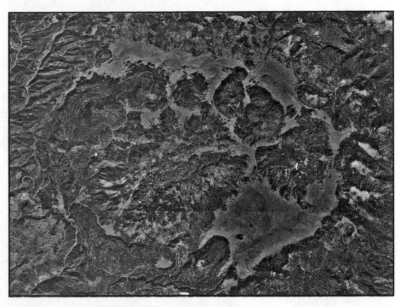

The circular nature of the Valles Caldera is apparent from this high altitude aerial photo. The caldera rim lies just outside the semicircle of the gray grasslands of the major valleys. Ring fracture domes arc from east to west in the northern quarter of the caldera. The distance from rim to rim is about fifteen miles.

nothing to support the weight of the overlying rock, a nine-mile wide plug of rock collapsed into the top of the magma chamber. Moving along the circular ring fractures, the material above the void dropped like a piston. The force of the piston and the sudden release of pressure pushed great quantities of fragmented magma out of the ring fractures. But before too long, the lower portion of the eruption column became choked with rock material and the weight of the plume could no longer be supported by the thrust of the escaping gases. The column collapsed from its own weight. With increasing speed, the gravity-driven mixture of scalding rock and gas hurtled toward the ground as a wave of pumice. Blown by gale-force winds, the collapsed column flowed outward and toward the east at speeds of up to 100 miles per hour, flowing through the canyons carved into the old volcanoes. Within minutes, the landscape near the canyons was completely devastated. Forests were covered with the thick flows and destroyed. Violent surges of hot ash poured over the pumice beds, whipping the surface into dunes. The pyroclastic flows from the collapse were not restricted to valleys, but radiated across the landscape as hot avalanches. Racing over the flanks of the older volcanoes, the flows formed a massive wedge of material—thick near the volcano and thinning at greater distances from the vent. Still hot as it settled in layers as much as 400 feet thick, the pyroclastic material fused to varying degrees. The rock formed is today called the Lower Bandelier Tuff or the Otowi Member of the Bandelier Tuff, named for a large pueblo ruin near some of its greatest exposures. It probably took no more than several hours for more than 65 cubic miles of rock fragments to be ejected from the ring fractures.

The ring fracture zone delineated a crater called the Toledo Caldera. Although it is almost circular in appearance, the collapse was asymmetric. The caldera was deeper to the east than the west as though the bottom had dropped down on a hinge like a huge trap door.

Within a matter of possibly hours and no more than days, the landscape of the Jemez volcanic field had radically changed.

Depleted of its high gas content, the magma chamber continued to erupt but in a less spectacular manner. Thick, viscous lavas flowed out of the ring fracture to form a semicircle of domes on the east and south sides of the caldera, which today include Rabbit Mountain and the Cerros de los Posos. These relatively quiet eruptions ruled the volcanic field for about the next 400,000 years.

But the magma rising at the intersection of the Rio Grande rift and the Jemez lineament had not yet finished its dramatic push toward the surface. At 1.2 million years ago, the entire violently eruptive sequence was repeated. Fresh ring fractures on a slightly smaller circle released about the same volume of magma, which again spread as pyroclastic flows beyond the walls of the original caldera. This second caldera, formed roughly on top of the first, is the Valles Caldera. Its massive ash flow deposits are called the Upper Bandelier Tuff or the Tshirege Member of the Bandelier Tuff, again named for a pueblo ruin.

Because it is today filled in by eroded sediments, the floor of the Valle Grande gives a deceptive picture of the violence of the collapse of the Valles Caldera. It is probable that the original floor of the crater was 3,000 feet lower than the Valle Grande today. The extent of the complete remaking of the Jemez landscape can be seen by the total amount of subsidence in the rocks beneath the volcanic pile. Under the nested calderas, the Precambrian basement rocks that were near the surface 16 million years before are now found at depths of around 15,000 feet. Immediately outside the caldera on Fenton Hill, the same rock is only 2,000 feet down.

The upward pressure exerted by the rising magma dome beneath the surface continued. Within 70,000 years of the Valles eruption, a central dome within the caldera had risen over 3,000 feet, a rate of more than 20 feet per year. That such a resurgent dome could rise with such speed seems fantastic. But a modern analog, the island of Iwo Jima off Japan, rises at an average rate of eight inches per year. Today, Redondo Peak stands high above the caldera floor, composed of a pile of Bandelier Tuff that erupted and fell within the caldera. Yet the hump-backed Redondo is only half of the resurgent dome. Sliced in half by the Redondo graben—a linear valley based in a series of faults—the true dome extends westward to the elongated ridge of Redondo Border.

"This story began with a tribute to the scenic beauty of the Valle Grande and then considered some of the titanic forces of volcanism with their own high dramas, but at the end it turned to the imagined beauty of a mountain lake. This circuit of interest is as it should be, for our goal has been a synthesis of a love for scenic beauty, some understanding of the story rocks may tell, and the drama of it all."

Clarence S. Ross, writing for New Mexico Magazine, *January 1962.*

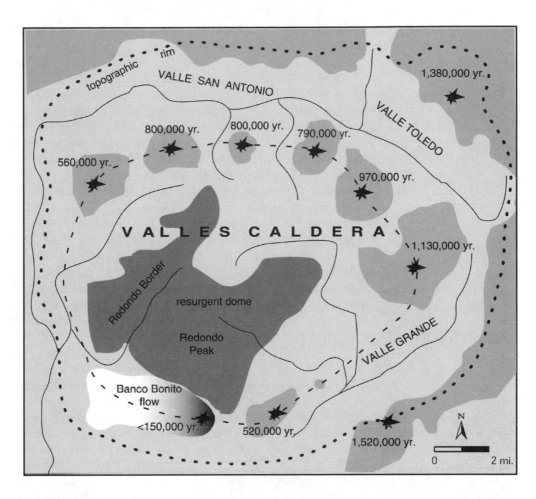

Between the resurgent dome and the walls of the caldera lies a circular depression called the moat. The ring fractures of the Valles Caldera lie within the moat. The circle inscribed by the ring fractures is nine miles in diameter; the topographic expression of the caldera across its rim is about 15 miles in diameter.

Continuing volcanic activity within the caldera occurred along the moat. The ring fractures tapped the magma chamber and permitted thick lava to reach the surface. These eruptions did not exhibit the violence of the caldera-forming ones but instead created lava domes that seemed to swell from the inside like yeast-risen bread dough. Around 1.1 million years ago, three such vents piled up rhyolite lava, and the conjoined domes formed Cerro del Medio, the hill that forms the northeastern backdrop to the Valle Grande. Some of these rhyolite flows cooled so rapidly that mineral crystals had no time to form. These flows produced a glassy-textured rock called obsidian. Over the next 600,000 years, successive ring-fracture domes erupted from east to west along the circle. The final dome-forming event gave rise to South Moun-

Outline map of the geologic features of the Valles Caldera. Dates show the temporal pattern of the eruptions of the ring fracture domes. The dotted line is the topographic rim of the caldera; the dashed line is the location of the ring fracture.

tain and its little brother Cerro La Jara, which today rises 200 feet above the floor of the Valle Grande.

The Valles Caldera played a significant role in the history of volcanology. In the late 1920s, young geologist Clarence Ross of the United States Geologic Survey rode horseback through the Jemez Mountains, mapping rock types and producing a comprehensive study of the range. In his evaluation of the processes that had developed the present landscape, Ross was the first to recognize the connection between large-volume ash flows and the formation of calderas. Up to that point, tuff deposits were subjects of much controversy among geologists: because tuffs have a layered appearance, some observers believed they were sediment deposits. Ross handed the research possibilities of the Jemez to his lead field assistant, Robert Smith, who with his assistant Roy Bailey continued into the 1980s to study, map, and refine the understanding of the Jemez and also the caldera-forming process. Ross and Smith's paper linking Bandelier Tuff to what they called the Jemez Caldera was a breakthrough in the study of volcanoes.[2]

The Valle Grande is is on the site of one of several lakes that formed within the Valles Caldera after the last massive explosive eruption of the volcano.

After the two major eruptions, the topographic expression of the caldera was that of a gigantic bowl. Precipitation falling within the bowl ran into the crater, but other than through evaporation, there was no way for the accumulating water to leave the bowl. With more water entering than could leave, over thousands of years the water level rose and great lakes filled the caldera. These first lakes within the caldera were the most extensive and probably covered the entire crater to a depth of several hundred feet. But within 100,000 years of the caldera-forming eruption, the lakes had drained. Outside the caldera rim, an ancestral stream that roughly followed the Jemez lineament slowly eroded a channel into the rim. Inside the crater, the rising resurgent dome displaced an equivalent volume of water, raising the lake level. At the lowest point on the rim, near where today's East Fork of the Jemez River meets the Cañon de San Diego, lake water spilled over the edge. Millions of gallons flowing through a narrow channel quickly eroded the breach into a deep canyon through the caldera rim and the colorful sedimentary rocks downstream. In terms of geologic time, the Cañon de San Diego formed with amazing speed.

The drainage pattern changed within the caldera with the ongoing formation of ring-fracture domes, damming the headwater streams to form small lakes. Lakes arose in the Valle Grande, Valle San Antonio, Valle Toledo, Valle Seco, Valle de los Posos, and on other small streams. Each of the grand *valles* of the caldera is found on former lakebeds. However, there is no simple explanation of why the open grasslands persist in these valleys instead of forests. Part of the answer lies in the soil. The calm waters of the lakes permitted over the years a slow settling of fine clay particles onto the lakebed. Compared with the coarse and rocky soils on the slopes of the caldera rim, the lakebed sediments were tightly compacted. Small streams deposited more sediments on top, creating soil that is dramatically different than that of the surrounding slopes. The valley soil makes it difficult for tree species to become established in the lowlands. Adding to this process, it may be that the colder air that settles in the valleys inhibits tree growth. Once they are thickly established, grasses effectively inhibit the growth of tree seedlings.

Cerro La Jara, the smallest of the ring-fracture domes in the Valles Caldera, rises above the fog on a summer morning. Redondo Peak, a towering resurgent dome, forms the skyline.

The most recent volcanic activity within the Valles Caldera occurred along the southern edge of the ring fracture. About 50,000 or 60,000 years ago, a small vent erupted, shooting ash skyward and creating beds of pumice up to 75 feet thick to the south and a small pyroclastic flow filling a valley pointing southwest. A small crater formed at the vent, known today as El Cajete (the washtub). After a brief lull, a vent about a mile north of El Cajete oozed a thick, obsidian-like lava in at least four separate eruptions. The lava, known as the Banco Bonito flow, spread four miles down a valley in the moat of the Valles Caldera and filled it with new rock.

The youngest rocks of the Valles Caldera eruptive sequence can be seen just west of the New Mexico Highway 4 crossing of the East Fork of the Jemez River near Jemez Falls Campground. North of the highway, a 100-foot cliff exposes South Mountain rhyolite at the base, a thick bed of blinding-white El Cajete pumice, and a top layer of black Banco Bonito obsidian. On the highway closer to Jemez Springs, the orange point of Battleship Rock is the result of the pyroclastic flow from El Cajete.

What is the current status of the magma that was the cause of this radical transformation of the Jemez region from a rift valley to volcanic mountains? Several lines of evidence indicate that one or more magma bodies still underlies the caldera. The lack of small earthquakes, an amplified subterranean heat flow, and the composition of gases that escape from the ground within the caldera all indicate the presence of magma. Other studies estimate that the pod of molten rock at the junction of the Rio Grande rift and the Jemez lineament lies only three miles beneath the caldera. Thus, the Valles Caldera is classified as one of three active calderas in the United States, and it has undoubtedly not finished its eruptive sequence.[3]

CHAPTER TWO
10,000 B.C. TO 1850

BEGINNINGS: THE PUEBLO
PEOPLE AND THE SPANISH ERA

In the oral tradition of the Jemez people—who in their own language are called the *Hemish*—the Creator directed the first people to emerge from the underworld at *Hoa-sjela*, a place now known as Stone Lake on the Jicarilla Apache Reservation in north-central New Mexico. The people made their homes in the area around the lake, extending their territory west to Largo Canyon. But hunting and gathering food in the dry mesa country was difficult, and raids by nomadic tribes made the area dangerous. During a winter solstice ceremony, Hemish caciques announced that the people would move south. For the next 300 years, the Hemish lived along ephemeral streams in the Gallina, New Mexico, area and spread as far south as La Ventana on the west side of the Nacimiento Mountains. However, after a time the people did not have adequate water for growing their crops. Once again, they were guided by instructions from the deities, who said that if the people went south they would find their new home in an area rich with resources. When they approached the proper place, an eagle would guide them the rest of the way. After a short journey along the mountains, the Hemish saw an eagle outlined on the highest peak of the range before them. Guided by the eagle, the people walked to their new home in the mountain range that today bears their name. The peak, called "the Father of the Northern Mountains," is now known as Redondo.[1]

Zia Pueblo has a similar tradition about the origin of their people and Zia residents also hold a deep reverence for the Jemez range. Their story of creation tells of the Zia people emerging from the underworld and migrating south. They stopped in the lush mountains near the foot of Redondo Peak and gathered their strength for a year, nurtured by the abundant game, fertile fields, and endless water found beneath the peak. However, the caciques believed that living at the origin of such natural riches would destroy the resources, so again the people moved south. They followed the river flowing from the foot of the peak to a place in the foothills of the mountains. On the flanks of the sacred mountains, the people built their new home, Zia Pueblo.

But the Zia people never forgot their ties to the central valleys of the Jemez Mountains. The modern pueblo has six ruling societies responsible for the health and welfare of the people. The names of the societies correspond to the names of the volcanic mounds found within the Valles Caldera. In the pueblo council, the heads of the societies sit in the same order as the hills, starting with Cerro del Medio and heading west to Cerro Seco.[2]

As other Pueblo groups settled in the foothills surrounding the Jemez Mountains, they too developed traditional and sacred ties to the Valles Caldera. Several non-Pueblo Native American groups, particularly the Navajo, also considered the Jemez country an important part of their homeland.

In the archeological record of New Mexico, the oldest sites—those dated from 11,500 to 7,500 years ago—are classified as the Paleo-Indian Period. Only one confirmed Paleo-Indian site has been discovered in the Jemez Mountains, although there likely are more. However, even in this early time, the superb quality of the raw materials for tool-making in the Valles Caldera attracted hunters to the great valleys. Obsidian—the dense, hard volcanic glass produced in abundance by the Jemez volcanoes—links the caldera with other archeological sites all over the western United States and must have been traded widely.

As the people of the ancestral cultures became more sedentary, distinct changes in tools and other crafts led to what archeologists call the Archaic Period. During this time, which began around 5500 B. C. and lasted to around 500 A.D., many family groups and clans established seasonal camps in the Valles Caldera. The people gathered in the caldera to hunt game, gather seeds and nuts, and collect obsidian and make tools. The camps were set along the edges of the grand valleys, near smaller meadows, and in saddles between major drainages throughout the central Jemez Mountains. From the camps, the people had nearby access to water, and the sites provided easy routes to a variety of habitats and thus a variety of foods. Site artifacts indicate that hunters sporadically occupied these campsites over the course of thousands of years.[3]

Starting around 500 A. D., the people of the Ancestral Pueblo culture began living in permanent housing. The first structures, simple pit houses, appear in the areas surrounding the Jemez Mountains and not in the range itself. Starting around 700 A.D., the first residents of the Jemez Mountains consolidated their villages into large pueblos near year-round water sources. In the summer the people fanned out into the surrounding mountains to grow their crops on fertile fields. On Banco Bonito, the site of the most recent volcanic flow in the range, the farmers found rich soils ideal for the short, high-mountain growing season. For shelter as they worked the fields, the farmers built one-room masonry field houses. Situated adjacent to the stands of corn and squash, these simple structures were built of rocks collected in the immediate area. The hard rhyolite was not suitable for shaping into building blocks, so the field houses are made of dry-stacked, irregularly shaped stones. Up to the summer of 2002, the remains of about 100 field houses had been discovered on Banco Bonito, indicating the importance of the lava flow-derived soils to

The fertile volcanic soils on the Banco Bonito lava flow attracted farmers who lived in the river valleys outside the Valles Caldera. The farmers came during the summer months and for shelter built small field houses near their crops. Dozens of field houses are located on Banco Bonito.

the farmers. Most of the field houses date from after 1350.[4]

As the Ancestral Pueblo culture of the Four Corners area drifted away in the years from 1200 to 1350, eight pueblo groups migrated east and settled in the foothills and plains surrounding the Jemez Mountains. Since their arrival, the people of these pueblos consider much of the Jemez Mountains their traditional domain. The mountains provided lands for procurement of food, materials for pottery, rock for tools, and the vital source of water for irrigation of their farms. Hunting parties scoured the

mountains for game; family groups gathered seeds and plants; ceremonial groups used the mountains for catching eagles and harvesting fir trees for use in ceremonies. In later times the pueblo people grazed their livestock in the valleys of the Valles Caldera. Herds were left to graze in the Valle Grande and the herders camped in the surrounding forests to protect the live-stock from the Navajos. The valleys of the Valles Caldera also served as the route of a trail from San Ildefonso to Jemez Pueblo.[5]

Obsidian is the thread that binds together the entire prehis-tory of the Valles Caldera. Formed by rapid cooling of silica-rich lava, obsidian has a glassy texture that holds a sharp, extremely thin edge on a broken surface. This ability to form the thinnest of edges makes obsidian an ideal material for creating stone knives, scrapers, and points. Skilled hunters can flake chips from quar-ried stone to produce tools as sharp as any steel instrument.

Attraction to Valles Caldera obsidian began as soon as native peoples arrived in New Mexico. Early hunters established obsid-ian quarries on the ring-fracture domes within the caldera. Work-ing with stone hammers—stout rocks without handles—the quarry workers broke up cobbles or nodules of obsidian that had

An obsidian bi-face artifact from the Valles Caldera. The length of the artifact is about 8 inches. Photo by Anastasia Steffen.

eroded from nearby cliff faces and boulders. They found the obisidian on the surface, in stream beds or gullies, and at the foot of cliffs. Quarries are recognized as extensive areas near the geologic source in which artifacts are found, and the sites often hold hammer stones and an abundance of worked chips. During the prehistory of the Jemez Mountains, Native Americans established three major obsidian quarries within the caldera: at Rabbit Mountain, on Cerro Toledo, and near Cerro del Medio. The obsidian flows of Cerro del Medio produced the largest and finest pieces of workable material. Some of the most concentrated quarrying took place along the northern border of the mountain and in a V-shaped meadow now known as Obsidian Valley.[6]

For archeologists each piece of obsidian holds two clues to the past. Obsidian contains about 0.2 percent water, but when a piece is fractured, the fresh surface begins to absorb moisture from the atmosphere. A water-rich hydration rind forms, the depth of which roughly corresponds to the length of the time the surface has been exposed to the air. Using a microscope, a technician can locate the diffusion front in a thin section sliced from an obsidian sample. By calibrating the depth of the rind with known environmental conditions, the amount of time since the surface was broken can be calculated and the age of a worked tool determined. Because of the richness of other opportunities for dating artifacts, obsidian hydration dating is rarely done in the Jemez, but the Jemez obsidian provides a wealth of base data for other areas.

Another signature ingrained in each flake of obsidian has allowed modern researchers to trace the prehistoric use of the rocks of the Valles Caldera. Each volcano erupts lava with a distinctive geochemical composition. Chemical analysis of the relative abundance of trace elements within lavas from known sources gives each volcano a unique, recognizable fingerprint. By matching a sample's composition to a chemical profile from a known source, any piece of obsidian can be matched to the source volcano.

Using geochemical signatures, archeologists discovered that obsidian material from the Valles Caldera quarries on Rabbit Mountain and Cerro del Medio traveled widely in prehistoric times. The excellent quality of Jemez obsidian made it the preferred material for making tools all over the region. Fine grains and the lack of gas pockets in the rock distinguished the caldera glass from other sources of material around the West. More than 80 percent of the obsidian in Archaic sites in New Mexico are from sources in the Jemez Mountains. Tools made from Valles Caldera obsidian have been uncovered in Blackwater Draw in eastern New Mexico and in a site 350 miles away in Wyoming. Carried by hand or in a pouch, one piece of Jemez volcanic glass was found at an ancient site in Leon County, Texas, over 700 miles from its source.[7]

The rounded stone to the left of the modern hammer is a stone hammer found at an obsidian quarry site near Cerro del Medio in the Valles Caldera. Photo by Anastasia Steffen.

In the mid-1500s, tales that the deserts and mountains in the unexplored territory north of Mexico were brimming with gold reached Spain. The first tentative European settlements were established in the Rio Grande Valley near the turn of the seventeenth century, and shortly thereafter Santa Fe, the capital of the colony of New Mexico, was founded. Searching for the rumored gold, the probing fingers of the advancing Spaniards reached from Santa Fe up the valley of the Jemez River. Soon soldiers crossed the mountains lying between Jemez Pueblo and the Rio Grande. Indeed, the first party to cross the range via the Valle Grande may have included the colonizer Juan de Oñate in the first years of the seventeenth century.[8]

The broad grasslands spread across the central Jemez region impressed these first Europeans in New Mexico. A 1779 map shows a vast open area surrounded by mountains that was given the prophetic name *Valle de los Bacas*, here probably meant to designate the Valley of the Cows. Later the grasslands were called the *Valles de Los Montaños*, the Valleys of the Mountains; the mountains to the east were dubbed the *Sierra de los Valles*, the Range of the Valleys. Before long, the largest of the valleys assumed the name of the Valle Grande, and collectively the grasslands were called *Los Valles*.[9]

After the arrival of the Spanish, the people of Jemez Pueblo maintained a herd of horses. The herd was considered to belong to the entire pueblo. As a valuable resource, it was placed in the hands of a war captain. During the spring and fall, the herd was taken to *Los Valles* for grazing. The captain appointed stockmen to watch the herd and to keep the rangeland from being overgrazed. In August the horses returned to the pueblo for the harvest season. During this time period, the pueblo people also grazed flocks of sheep in the valleys of the Jemez Mountains.

The Valles Caldera falls within the traditional lands of many of the pueblos surrounding the Jemez Mountains, including the San Ildefonso, San Juan, Santa Ana, Santa Clara, Santo Domingo, and Tesuque pueblos. Sharing the Jemez landscape with the pueblo people and the newcomer Spanish were the nomadic tribes living to the north and west. Jicarilla Apache people often used the caldera for hunting grounds. The Utes only occasionally entered the Jemez Mountains, but the Navajo routinely used the range, and especially the Valle Grande, as a route connecting their homelands to the Rio Grande Valley. Through the 1880s, Navajo raiding parties rustled sheep from ranchers along the Rio Grande and herded them back to the mountains of western New Mexico through the heart of the Jemez.[10]

CHAPTER THREE
1851 TO 1864

AMERICAN MILITARY ACTIONS ON THE JEMEZ FRONTIER

In 1846 American General Stephen Watts Kearny invaded New Mexico and conquered its capital without firing a shot. His army marched down the Santa Fe Trail from Kansas, entered Santa Fe, and encountered no serious resistance from the Mexican government. Encouraged by the ease of his victory, Kearny hustled west to claim California, leaving behind a small force to keep order and protect the residents of what he correctly assumed would soon become a part of the United States. However, his casual victory was deceptive; before a year passed, the citizens of Taos would rebel, killing Kearny's appointee to the governorship, Charles Bent.

Kearny left behind a company of American soldiers and charged them with reducing Indian raids within New Mexico. As a base of operations, Kearny directed his quartermaster, Captain Randolph Marcy, to construct a small fort on a ridge that overlooked the plaza at Santa Fe. Fort Marcy—not named for its

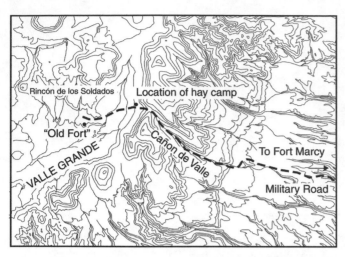

Rincón de los Soldados

Location of hay camp

"Old Fort"

VALLE GRANDE

Cañon de Valle

To Fort Marcy

Military Road

The military road from Santa Fe to the Valle Grande traversed the Pajarito Plateau before climbing through Cañon de Valle to a pass leading to the upper Valle Grande. Nesbit and Parker's hay camp was located about 50 yards from the edge of the forest at the western foot of the pass. The road continued to the vicinity of the "Old Fort."

builder but for then-Secretary of War William L. Marcy—was completed in 1847. From this base Missouri volunteers under the command of Colonel Alexander Doniphan found themselves charged with the monumental task of trying to check the frequent raids by Navajos and Apaches on the settlements along the Rio Grande and in other parts of New Mexico.

In 1851 drought conditions in the Southwest made it difficult for the military detachment at Santa Fe to obtain sufficient hay for their numerous stock animals. The normal channel for acquiring feed was for the quartermaster to make a casual purchase from whoever offered feed for sale. But with offers and supplies dwindling with the scant rainfall, the Army post turned to contractors to cut and dry native grass and deliver it to the fort. In one of the first contracts, the quartermaster at Fort Marcy hired Robert Nesbit and Hiram R. Parker to cut hay for the Army livestock. With the going price for hay hauled over 25 miles at $50 per ton, the two Santa Fe residents hoped to make what at the time could become a small fortune.[1]

Nesbit and Parker looked to the high-elevation valleys of the Jemez Mountains as their source of grass, that "being the only place in the whole country where grass could be had on account of the excessive dryness of the season." Recognizing the potential value of the hay enterprise in the Valle Grande, the Army provided material and labor to improve portions of the road between Santa Fe and the Valle Grande. The road crossed the Rio Grande at what would later become Buckman, climbed Mortandad Canyon to the Pajarito Plateau, and used Cañon de Valle as passage over the crest of the Sierra de los Valles.[2]

In early summer Nesbit and Parker set up camp near the head of the Valle Grande. Their hay camp sat on the west flank of the Sierra de los Valles below the pass the Pueblos called "water reservoir gap," which was named for the small but persistent natural ponds at the summit. The camp was located in a grassy alcove surrounded by huge ponderosa pines; to the west were the unlimited grasses of the Valle Grande. The partners built a small fort of "bottom wood" logs. On the side of the fort that faced the pines, they constructed a 30-by-50-foot corral to hold the sizable mule train that would haul the abundant hay cuttings back to Santa Fe. Nesbit and Parker stacked four or five cottonwood logs to build four-foot high walls. Not anticipating any trouble, Nesbit and Parker left no openings in the fort except one on the side facing the corral.

On the afternoon of July 1, 1851, a typical summer rainstorm hit the camp and a light drizzle persisted through the evening. Nesbit and Parker posted two guards, but the sentries found it difficult to "see twenty steps from where they were walking." About one o'clock that night, an arrow whistled out of the darkness and pierced the neck of one of the guards assigned to watch the corral. The injured man cried out, fired his gun, and instantly a shower of arrows was unleashed from the darkness into the fort. A moment later, the entire camp was awake and the men ready to fight for their lives. Nesbit estimated that 250 to 300 Navajos surrounded them. Most of the hay camp workers were pinned inside the fort by a "continuous stream of arrows." (It was later noted that about 50 arrows were stuck in the door.) Through the one window of the fort, Parker fired two shots from his revolver toward the pines beyond the corral, but the opening was so high that he couldn't see where his shots were going. For more than two hours the few men outside the fort fought off the Navajos. Just before dawn the raiders brought down part of the corral and made off with 43 mules and 6 horses. The only casualty was the slightly wounded camp guard shot at the beginning of the attack.

Later that morning Nesbit wrote a letter to Colonel John Munroe at Santa Fe and requested immediate assistance. To investigate Nesbit's claims, Munroe dispatched Lieutenant Beverly H. Robertson from the army post at Abiquiu, which was about 10 miles north of the hay camp. As Robertson and his patrol entered the Valle Grande, they spotted a group of Indians herding stock on the opposite side of the valley. Assuming that the Indians were Navajos about to again attack the hay camp, Robertson ordered his men to open fire. The Native Americans immediately rushed on horseback across the valley toward the soldiers, frantically making signs of friendship. Robertson recognized the riders as being from Jemez Pueblo and ceased fire before anyone was hurt.

The Jemez Pueblo group had pursued the Navajo raiders the morning after the attack. Catching up with the raiders on the border of Navajo country, they had attacked them, killing two men and recapturing five mules, and were on their way to the hay camp to return the mules to their owners. The Jemez people told Robertson the number of Navajos in the raiding party was between 30 and 40. Robertson continued to the hay camp and verified what he could about the attack. Although he found Nesbit's account of the battle somewhat exaggerated, Robertson thought the camp would benefit from additional protection. However, Col. Munroe felt that the army camp at Abiquiu was close enough to provide protection to the hay cutters.[3]

In the end, the lack of military protection was irrelevant. As Nesbit and Parker's mule trains hauled the hay from camp over

"...at about one o'clock in the morning there was a large band of Navajo Indians supposed to be from two hundred and fifty to three hundred made an attack upon our camp and corrall - the house in which we lived being built of logs and in the most substantial manner...[it] was still drissiling, so that it was almost impossible for the men on guard to see twenty steps from where they were walking - so that the first salutation or intination of the approach of the Indians, was an arrow shot into the neck of one of the sentinels, accompanied by a yeall and a shower of arrows..."

Letter from Nesbit and Parker to Col. Munroe, July 2, 1851.

The 1851 hay camp was located near this stand of old-growth ponderosa pine in the upper Valle Grande.

"There were no guns fired at the Indians, except one, by the sentinel on Post. The sentinel said it was impossible from the darkness of the night, to tell their exact number, but he believed there could not have been less than forty."

Lt. Beverly H. Robertson, reporting to his commanding officer on the attack.

the rough route to Santa Fe, the hungry animals ate most of the supply of feed before they arrived at their destination.[4]

Undaunted by the presence of the American force at Santa Fe and counter to proclamations from the military that the Navajo frontier was secure, Navajo raiders continued their attacks on the farms and ranches of northern New Mexico, including those in the Jemez Mountains. In 1853 Navajos killed two sheepherders at Vallecito on Oso Creek, a few miles northeast of the Valle Grande. In 1856 400 sheep owned by Jose Ignacio Montoya were stolen and two herders killed. The New Mexican militia gave chase to the raiders. In the Valle Grande the party caught up with four Navajos herding the stolen sheep. A small battle erupted, leaving two Navajos dead.[5]

Throughout the early American occupation of New Mexico, the military leaders repeatedly but unsuccessfully sought to make peace with the Navajos. The task of banishing the Navajos to a reservation would fall to a man who arrived in New Mexico in 1862 expecting to fight a Confederate army, but whose major struggles were with Native Americans. At the start of the Civil War, Major James Henry Carleton was commander of Company K at Fort Tejon in southern California. Born in Maine, Carleton received his fighting experience by serving as aide-de-camp for General John Wool during the Mexican War. He received honors for his bravery at the Battle of Buena Vista and was promoted to captain. After continuing his service in northern New Mexico and southern Colorado through the 1850s, Carleton was sent to California. Union military strategists ordered him and his command of volunteer soldiers to New Mexico in late 1861, directing the California Column to repel the threat of a Confederate takeover in New Mexico. Carleton efficiently made his way east, making quick work of weak Confederate resistance in Arizona, and was in Santa Fe by the summer of 1862.

Once New Mexico was secure from the Confederates, the Army assigned Carleton the task of keeping Kearny's 1846 promise that New Mexico settlements would be safe from Indian attack. In a characteristic no-nonsense, no-discussion manner, Carleton decided to relocate the Apaches and the Navajos on a 1,600 square-mile reservation along the Pecos River. The central feature of the reservation gave it the name Bosque Redondo.

Captain William McCleave defeated the main band of Mescalero Apaches near Alamogordo, and Carleton ordered them to the Bosque Redondo reservation. In the north Carleton hired Kit Carson as his field commander for the Navajo campaign. Carson pursued the Navajos into the Canyon de Chelly area. The campaign ended in the deep snows of winter and the Navajos were forced to march to Bosque Redondo.

Neither the Apaches nor the Navajos felt a connection with the landscape of the reservation. They resisted being sent to their designated home on the Pecos, and once there small bands continually slipped away. To discourage escape from the reservation, Carleton sought to block the routes between Bosque Redondo and the Apache and Navajo homelands in the northwest part of New Mexico. One of the most important escape routes traversed north-south through the Valle Grande.

On August 17, 1863, Carleton assembled a detachment commanded by Lieutenant Erastus W. Wood and ordered them to set up a camp in the Valle Grande. Accompanying Wood were five noncommissioned officers and 31 privates from Company A, 1st Infantry, California Volunteers. Carleton's orders were simple, direct, and brutal. The soldiers were to head to the Valles "and there, in that vicinity, to lie in wait for thirty days, to kill every Navajo or Apache Indian who attempts to go through that noted thoroughfare. No women and children will be harmed; these will be captured."

On September 27, Lieutenant P. A. J. Russell, with four of the California Volunteers and a party of Pueblo people, rode from Camp Valles Grandes to follow the trail of a band of Navajos suspected of stealing stock from villages on the Rio Grande. Russell's command surprised the Navajos at Jemez Springs and, following Carleton's orders, killed eight men, captured twenty women and children, and recovered sheep and horses.[6]

The soldiers stayed at Camp Valles Grandes through the first snows of autumn, supposedly long enough to leave plenty of traces of their encampment. However, the whereabouts of Camp Valles Grandes has puzzled modern researchers. Maps from 1876 through the 1930s indicate an "old fort" near the springs at the head of the East Fork of the Jemez River. Some students of history speculated that the camp was located at the site of the Nesbit and Parker hay camp. Another clue—or source of confusion—is that an idyllic alcove in the grasslands of the upper Valle Grande is named the Rincón de los Soldados, the "corner of the soldiers." Neither the reputed "old fort" nor the hay camp lies within the Rincón de los Soldados.

John Davenport, ranch manager for the Bond family in the first half of the twentieth century, saw the remains of the fort when he worked the ranch in the 1920s. At that time Davenport could see that the structure was solidly built with logs three feet in diameter. In 1959 Davenport said the fort was long gone, but he left no clues as to the location of the fort. Since that time, several groups have attempted to locate the remains of the fort without success.[7]

The "Old Fort" is marked on every map of the Baca Location No. 1 drawn from 1876 to 1934. From Edgar Hewitt's Archeological Map of a Portion of the Jemez Plateau of New Mexico, 1910.

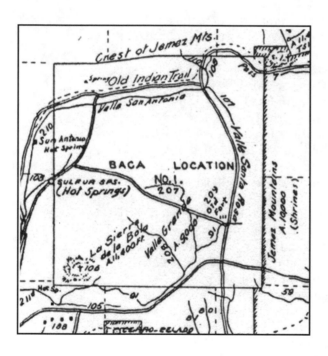

CHAPTER FOUR
1860 TO 1899

THE LUIS MARIA CABEZA DE BACA LAND GRANT

During their rule of the Southwest, the Spanish and Mexican governments issued hundreds of land grants to settlers in the colony of New Mexico. The Luis Maria Cabeza de Baca Land Grant is unique in two ways. It is the only land grant that does not include any of its original acreage, and it is the only grant that is scattered across three states. Eventually fragmented in five parcels, the roots of the Valles Caldera National Preserve lie in this anomaly among land claims.[1]

From the time he served as alcalde (judge) of Santo Domingo Pueblo in 1792 until his death at the hands of a Mexican soldier in 1827, Luis Maria Cabeza de Baca was never far from controversy. His propensity for trouble had far-reaching effects beyond his premature demise: Luis Maria's aggressiveness played a primary role in the formation of the Valles Caldera National Preserve. That a single parcel of land nearly 100,000 acres in size was still available into the late twentieth century can be traced directly to this early Cabeza de Baca.

Luis Maria Cabeza de Baca had a rich pedigree in both the Old and New Worlds. His ancestors were hard-working peasants with close ties to the landscape in the mountainous Jerez de la Fronta in southern Spain. In 1212, during the Spanish wars with the Moors, a shepherd named Martin Alhaja gave simple but important service to the Spanish king. The Moors blocked the mountain passes, but Alhaja showed the king's force an alternate route around the strongly entrenched enemy and gave the victory to the Spanish. The commoner is said to have marked his route with the skull of a cow. The king rewarded Alhaja by elevating him to the nobility, and the new nobleman changed his name to Cabeza de Vaca, the head of a cow.[2]

From their home in nearby Peña Blanca, the Cabeza de Baca family herded some of their sheep in the well-watered grasslands of the Jemez Mountains from as early as the 1820s.

The New Mexico Cabeza de Baca was a distant cousin of Alvar Nunez Cabeza de Baca, one of the first Spaniards to see the interior of the Southwest—although not exactly of his own accord. This Cabeza de Baca and three companions roamed from Florida to Sonora, Mexico, as captives of Native Americans. The quartet began their journey as part of a stranded gold-hunting party in Florida in 1528. After constructing boats of timber and horse hides, the treasure hunters hoped to follow the coastline of the Gulf of Mexico to the Spanish settlements in Mexico. Storms and misfortune scattered the group, but four, including Cabeza de Baca, struggled ashore and banded together. Almost immediately, the local native residents captured the group. As captives Cabeza de Baca and his companions spent eight years wandering through the Southwest, seeking a way to get home. In 1536 they drifted into a town on the northwest fringe of Spanish rule in Mexico. They brought with them wild tales of treasures in the interior of the southwest that set off the Spanish *entradas* into what became New Mexico.

Luis Maria Cabeza de Baca was born in Santa Fe in 1754. His father, Juan Antonio Baca, descended from Cristobal Baca, one of the second wave of colonizers that joined Juan Oñate during the initial Spanish colonization attempt of New Mexico. Luis Maria was a soldier stationed at Santa Fe in 1777 when he married his first of three wives, Maria Lopez. At the time he was described as a man of average stature, black-haired and fair-skinned, with no beard and with a scar over his right eye. In 1803 Luis Maria demonstrated his yearning for prestige by signing his name "Cabeza de Baca," which he expanded back to the original from his father's simple "Baca."[3]

In 1818 Luis Maria, along with his third wife and extensive family of 17 surviving children, lived near the village of Peña Blanca. The family had purchased a 25,000-acre ranch along the Rio Grande from Cochiti Pueblo. It was not a peaceful coexistence, however, and the Pueblo tried to annul its sale of land to Cabeza de Baca by claiming he had used intimidation and fraud to induce them to sell. The people of Cochiti Pueblo won the ensuing lawsuit in 1819, but Cabeza de Baca refused to vacate the land—nor did he ever leave the ranch he claimed was his own. (The matter was finally settled by an act of Congress in 1983 when the land was returned to the pueblo.) Instructive as to the man's character, this was Cabeza de Baca's second brush with the law. In 1792 Luis Maria was the object of a lawsuit brought by Santo Domingo Pueblo, which charged that he abused his position as alcalde and mistreated the residents of the pueblo.[4]

A summer storm passes over the Valle Toledo.

As the sheep industry rapidly expanded in the early nineteenth century, grazing land along the major river valleys including the Rio Grande came under increasing pressure. Ranchers along the rivers looked elsewhere for new grazing lands. Cabeza de Baca used his time in military service and his favored name to acquire prime land for his growing flocks. To add to his landholdings in Peña Blanca, he applied to the Spanish government for two land grants. His first efforts were focused on lands in and around the Jemez Mountains near his home. He petitioned the government for the Ojo de Espiritu Santo Grant, which was located on a parcel of land west of the Jemez Mountains. The land had been granted to the Zia, Jemez, and Santa Ana Pueblos in 1766, but Luis Maria claimed it had been abandoned by the grantees. Indeed, continual raids by Navajos had kept the owners from using the grant, but in the end Cabeza de Baca would fare no better. He received title to the grant on May 24, 1815, but within five years was driven off the property by the Navajos.[5]

Cabeza de Baca next turned his attention to territory beyond the borders of Spanish settlement and to the edge of the Great Plains east of the Sangre de Cristo Mountains. Serving for a time as alcalde of San Miguel del Bado, Luis Maria was aware of the great pastures along the Gallinas River. His acquaintance Antonio Ortiz alerted him to the richness of the land just north of Ortiz's grant on the Pecos River. In January 1821 Cabeza de Baca petitioned the Provincial Deputation in Durango, Mexico, for a grant of land at Las Vegas Grandes. In his initial grant request, Cabeza de Baca presented himself as one of nine petitioners, but he later resubmitted the petition as an individual, claiming that the other petitioners had lost interest in the grant. In its final version, the request was for Luis Maria and seventeen sons, some of whom were actually sons-in-law.

Because of unsettled conditions on the Mexican frontier, Cabeza de Baca did not make his request before the Governor of New Mexico, but instead went the higher authorities in Durango, Mexico. The Provincial Deputation president Diego Garcia Conde and secretary Miguel de Zubirria approved the grant request on May 29, 1821. New Mexico governor Facundo Melgares supported the grant petition.

Cabeza de Baca sought to exploit the lush grasslands crossed by flowing streams fed by the mountains to the west. To this end, he set the original boundaries of the grant as "...on the north, the Chapellote River; on the east, the Aguage de la Llequa and the Antonio Ortiz Grant; on the south, the San Miguel de Vado Grant; and on the west, the summit of the Pecos Mountains." The grant, known as the Luis Maria Cabeza de Baca or the Las Vegas Grandes Land Grant, encompassed more than a half-million acres and was among the largest awarded by the Mexican government.[6]

The alcalde at San Miguel de Bado, the closest settlement to the new land grant, was instructed to place Cabeza de Baca in possession of the land. However, in a period of relative calm with the Plains Indians, settlers from San Miguel de Bado were using the area of the grant for grazing sheep and cattle. The San Miguel de Bado alcalde stalled for two years, but pressure from the governor finally stirred the alcalde into permitting Cabeza de Baca to use the land.

Just how much the eighteen males of the Cabeza de Baca family actually used the Luis Maria Cabeza de Baca Grant has long been in dispute. Luis Maria probably never left Peña Blanca and left the management of the grant to his sons, particularly his eldest, Juan Antonio. In 1831 Josiah Gregg recorded in his journal:

> At Gallinas Creek we found a large flock of sheep grazing upon the adjacent plain; while a little hovel at the foot of a cliff showed it to be a rancho. A swarthy ranchero soon made his appear-

"Don Luis Maria Cabeza de Baca, resident of the Provence of New Mexico, for himself and in the name of seventeen male children, appears before the Supreme Tribunal of the Deputation of the Provence of New Mexico, to who corresponds the distribution and marking of Public lands, and states that a certain tract of land suitable for cultivation and pasturage, called the Vegas Grandes on the Gallina River in the jurisdiction of El Bado, being in the above condition, and not having sufficient room, and being very much confined, I suffer a great many injuries."

Luis Maria Cabeza de Baca, from a translation of the original grant petition, 1821.

ance from whom we procured a treat of goat's
milk, with some dirty ewe's milk 'curdle cheese' to
supply the place of bread.[7]

The sheepherder encountered by Gregg was probably one of Luis
Maria's sons, who lived in a hut at Loma Montosa.

The death of Luis Maria made it more difficult for the family
to continually occupy the grant. A frequently told version of his
death states that in 1827 a party of American trappers led by
Ewing Young headed north after a winter of collecting beaver
pelts along the tributaries of the Gila River in southern New
Mexico. Just prior to this journey, the Mexican government at
Santa Fe decided to crack down on foreign trappers in New
Mexico, and Young received word of the change in attitude as he
traveled toward Taos along the Rio Grande. To help Young, Luis
Maria Cabeza de Baca agreed to hide thirteen packs of pelts on
his property in Peña Blanca. However, one of Young's party
informed Governor Manuel Armijo of
the illegal cache and on May 16
Armijo sent nine soldiers to Peña
Blanca to seize the furs. Luis Maria
refused to surrender the contraband
pelts and went so far as to fire a
number of shots at the military party.
When the Mexican soldiers returned
fire, Luis Maria was seriously wounded. His will, dated May 28, 1827,
indicates that his condition quickly
deteriorated and shortly thereafter
Luis Maria died.[8]

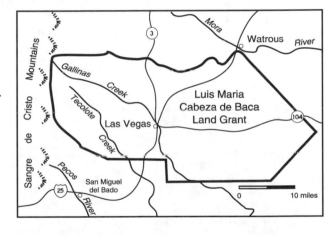

During the late 1820s and early
1830s, the family may have intermit-
tently run as many as 3,000 sheep on
their land grant. When they felt secure from Indian raids, the
family stayed at Las Vegas Grandes. Around 1833 the family
abandoned the grant, citing raids by the Pawnees that drove off
600 horses and mules. No evidence exists that any attempt was
made to irrigate the land.[9]

In 1835 Luis Maria's eldest son, Juan Antonio, was killed
while shepherding in the Jemez Mountains. The Cabeza de Baca
family regrouped, leaving the Las Vegas Grandes grant unoccu-
pied. Meanwhile, an increased military presence on the eastern
frontier of New Mexico led to quieter times and few Indian raids.
By 1834 the population of San Miguel de Bado was on the rise, and
settlers were expanding their grazing lands into the Las Vegas
area. In 1835, after several years of trying, a group of thirty
settlers was awarded a grant in the Las Vegas area with similar

*Modern features
make the immense
size of the Cabeza
de Baca land grant
apparent. The
property reached
from the summit of
the Sangre de Cristo
Mountains out onto
over 30 miles of the
Great Plains and
stretched about 25
miles north to south.*

boundaries to the Cabeza de Baca family's Las Vegas Grandes grant. Despite the similarities of the grants, and believing reports that the family had abandoned the property, the Santa Fe government approved the Las Vegas Community grant.

The grant was made available to all residents of San Miguel who lacked land. It was a typical community land grant: small private holdings were to be occupied, with water and pastures held in common. The name Baca appears among those who received allotments, and some of these may have been children or grandchildren of Luis Maria Cabeza de Baca. Although it was 1838 before a permanent settlement was made at Las Vegas, by the time the American invasion under General Stephen Kearny arrived in 1846, the newcomers had established a thriving community.[10]

As part of the postwar settlement between the United States and Mexico in 1848, the Treaty of Guadalupe Hidalgo promised the new American citizens of the territory that all land grants from the Spanish and Mexican governments would be evaluated and, if found to be valid, honored. In 1854, to stimulate settlement in New Mexico, Congress authorized donations of 160 acres of land to any citizen who occupied and improved the land over a period of four years. This necessitated the clear delineation of land grants within the territory. On July 22, 1854, Congress established the

Tomas Dolores Cabeza de Baca (left) was one of the grandsons of Luis Maria Cabeza de Baca who challenged the legality of the Las Vegas Community Land Grant. His older brother, Francisco Tomas Cabeza de Baca, led the family's attempts to reach a settlement over the disputed Las Vegas Land Grant. Courtesy of the Museum of New Mexico, Neg. No. 48003

position of Surveyor General of New Mexico and appointed Texan William Pelham to the post. Pelham was charged with determining the validity of all grant claims.

Finding few official Spanish and Mexican records in Santa Fe, William Pelham required all grant holders to submit title documents. This call for documentation opened up the opportunity for legal battles, fraud, and the eventual wresting of many of the lands in question from the hands of the legitimate title holders and into the hands of Anglo-Americans who were quick to take advantage of the situation.

When the Surveyor General began operations in Santa Fe in 1854, it is unclear how much the Cabeza de Baca family felt they had claim to the Las Vegas land grant. In 1837 Francisco Tomas Cabeza de Baca, the eldest of Luis Maria's grandsons, wrote a letter to Governor Armijo protesting the issuance of the Las Vegas Community Grant. Even in 1854, the family could argue that they never truly abandoned the grant. Francisco Tomas Cabeza de

Baca (who went by the name Tomas) sought legal counsel to help
lead him through the maze of required paperwork, which was
written in a language many of his family members barely understood, to obtain title. It is possible, however, that the family was
approached by a lawyer who saw an opportunity for profiting
from the unsettled land grant claim. In either case, the Cabeza de
Baca family hired attorney John S. Watts to handle the legal
work.[11]

John S. Watts was one of a small group of lawyers who
arrived in Santa Fe during the years immediately following the
American conquest of New Mexico. Watts hailed from Indiana
where he was a political friend of Abraham Lincoln. He arrived in
Santa Fe shortly after New Mexico became an American territory,
ready to accept an appointment as a territorial judge. As he
traveled the long road from Missouri, the political winds of
Washington changed and Watts found that his appointment had
been revoked. Quickly assessing the possibilities in the new
territory, Watts refocused his energy to specializing on land
claims for grantees or their heirs. Watts did the legal legwork,
researching land titles, interviewing the claimants, and writing
complex briefs in support of the claims. Working closely with the
Surveyor General's office and using his gained position of territorial delegate to Congress to full advantage, over the next 20 years
Watts would be a part of 43 of a total of 53 private land grant
cases in New Mexico.[12]

Whether Watts approached the family or the heirs of Luis
Maria initiated the contact, in 1854 the Cabeza de Baca family
hired Watts to make their claim on the Luis Maria Cabeza de Baca
Land Grant. Tomas Cabeza de Baca was the leader of the 21 heirs
who participated in the suit. Watts realized that a quick move on a
large land grant case would have a greater chance of success to
pass through Congress and immediately went to work on the
claim. At the same time the Las Vegas community hired lawyers to
work toward confirmation of their grant. Since the community
grant had been awarded, the town had grown to hold more than
2,000 residents. Because of the complications and the number of
people involved, both grant cases took several years to prepare.

Surveyor General Pelham received the Brief of Claimants
from Watts in 1858. Rather than just submit the legal documents
and wait for a ruling, Watts made what amounts to a preemptive
strike. The attorney was clever enough to figure that Congress, at
the time heavily preoccupied with the issues of slavery and
secession, might be unwilling to let the courts decide the matter
and possibly displace 2,200 people. Watts told the Surveyor
General that the Cabeza de Baca family would be willing to waive
their claim in exchange for an equivalent acreage elsewhere.
Pelham was a careful judge of the facts, taking his time to weigh
all the evidence. In early 1860 he ruled that both the Cabeza de

*"It is not the wish
of the present
claimants to disturb
the present intrud-
ers upon their
property on the
confirmation of
their grant. They
will be content with
the privilege of
selecting of the
public lands...a
quantity of land
equal to their grant
rather than be
annoyed or annoy
others with lengthy
and expensive
lawsuits...."*

*John Watts in the
Brief of the Claim-
ants, 1858.*

Baca and Las Vegas Community grants were valid. Rather than decree a resolution to the situation, Pelham said, "proper tribunals would sort it out."[13]

Congress confirmed the decision to validate both claims on June 21, 1860. However, the legislative body was left with the dilemma of the situation evolving into a protracted legal battle or taking a serious look at Watts' proposed alternative. Congress jumped—or was subtly pushed—at the chance for such an amiable settlement.[14]

In the settlement legislation, Congress declared "that it shall be lawful for the heirs of Luis Maria Baca, who make claim to the same tract of land as is claimed by the Town of Las Vegas, to select, in lieu of the land claimed by them, an equal quantity of vacant land, not mineral, in the Territory of New Mexico, to be located by them in square bodies, not exceeding five in number." The heirs of Luis Maria were given three years to make their selection of equivalent land. In 1860 the Territory of New Mexico included all of Arizona and part of southern Colorado. The Cabeza de Baca family had about 250,000 square miles from which to choose and had at their disposal some of the richest lands available in the Southwest.[15]

Before the alternative lands could be selected, the Surveyor General had to survey the original Luis Maria Cabeza de Baca Land Grant to determine its size. Completed in the fall of 1860, the survey found the Cabeza de Baca family entitled to 496,446 acres of land. The five parcels were to be called the Baca Locations or Floats, and each would be nearly 100,000 acres.

On December 11, 1860, Surveyor General A. P. Wilbar certified that he had received a formal request from the heirs of Luis Maria Cabeza de Baca to locate their first tract of land at the "Valles Grandes."

> *Approved June 21st, 1860, a tract of Land one fifth the area of the Grant of Las Vegas which said Legal Representative Baca selected at the Valles Grandes, and vicinity to be square in form, vacant*

The Cabeza de Baca family stipulated that the first float be located in the rich valleys of the central Jemez Mountains not far from their family's roots in Peña Blanca. As the grazing lands along the Rio Grande grew crowded, the Cabeza de Baca family had looked to the canyons and mesas of the Jemez Mountains. For more than 50 years, whenever the Navajo situation permitted it, the family grazed sheep in the range. Indeed, Juan Antonio Cabeza de Baca, son of Luis Maria, had been killed in the mountains while grazing his sheep in 1835. The men of the family undoubtedly knew of the central valleys of the range. Thus, the Baca Location Number 1 was selected to encompass the rich grasslands, surrounded on all sides by forested peaks, of the Valle Grande, the Valle Toledo, and the Valle San Antonio. The Surveyor General's office in Santa Fe approved the application by Tomas Cabeza de Baca, the legal representative of the heirs of Luis Maria Cabeza de Baca, on December 11, 1860.[16]

The family gave John Watts the job of selecting the other four square parcels of land. Watts made his choices with a trained eye on their potential for raising livestock. All were lush grass-lands situated to take maximum advantage of rivers and streams. The Baca Float Number 2 was located on the plains of eastern New Mexico, not far north of the present Tucum-cari. The Canadian River split the property in two, and guaranteed a supply of water to the land and its owners. Two floats were in Arizona: Number 3 lay just north of Nogales near the old mission of Tumacacori and along the Santa Cruz River; and further north, Number 5 sat on the Tonto Rim north of Prescott. Watts turned to southern Colorado and the San Luis Valley for Baca Float Num-ber 4, located along the foot of the Sangre de Cristo Mountains.[17]

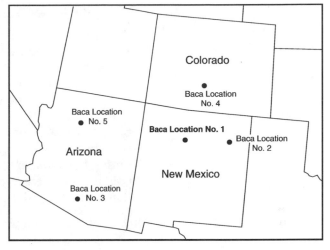

As payment for his years of services to the Baca family, Watts received outright the ownership of three of the floats, the Baca Locations No. 2, 3, and 4. In 1871 Watts rounded up the signatures of 86 Baca heirs and purchased from them their interests in Baca Location No. 5 for $6,800. Wheeling and dealing in real estate, Watts quickly added to his fortune: two years after he acquired it, Watts sold the Baca Location No. 5 for $30,000. Using his influence as an experienced attorney and as a large landowner, Watts became a member of the Supreme Court of New Mexico and eventually retired to his home in Indiana free from financial worry.[18]

The locations of the five Baca Floats in Colorado, Arizona, and New Mexico.

The Cabeza de Baca family's selection of the Baca Location No. 1 set the basic boundaries of the Valles Caldera National Preserve, and its placement under private ownership made possible, more than a century later, the availability of a nearly 100,000-acre block of land for transfer into the public domain.

The wheels of bureaucracy have always turned at a glacial pace. Congress approved the compromise solution for the con-flicting claims over the Luis Maria Cabeza de Baca Land Grant in 1860, but the Civil War forced the family to wait while the nation's attention was elsewhere. The processes of finalizing the legal issues and surveying the land were not completed for 16 years. John Watts restated the family's request for the boundary survey in 1870; the Acting Land Commissioner instructed the Surveyor General in Santa Fe to make the survey in May 1871. Further delays postponed the legal recording of the Baca Location No. 1 boundaries until 1876. In the summer of that year, U. S. Deputy

Surveyors McBroom and Sawyer marked the land grant boundaries with stones, small monuments, and blazes on aspen and pine trees. The surveyors claimed to accomplish the task of delineating the grant boundaries in rugged terrain in only four days in June 1876. They concluded their report with a general description of the property:

> [The property] is finely adapted for stock growing, raising a fine rank growth of grass especially in the interior which is filled with several small valleys and fine streams containing myriads of trout. The soil in the valley is rich but on account of its Altitude is too cold to raise any kind of grain or vegetables. There are no settlers living upon the Grant. Large herds of sheep are kept here during the summer, but not during winter as the cold is too severe...The Grant contains an abundance of pine and aspen timber.[19]

Only after defining markers encircled the property was the family permitted to take possession of the grant. By the late 1870s, an increased military presence in New Mexico and the extra protection afforded by the Army made it possible for ranchers to run large flocks of sheep in the mountains, but not all family members wanted to use the Baca Location No. 1 as their range. Francisco Tomas Cabeza de Baca and other family members remained in Peña Blanca, which was only a dozen miles by trail

Luis Maria Cabeza de Baca had a succession of three wives and produced 24 offspring.

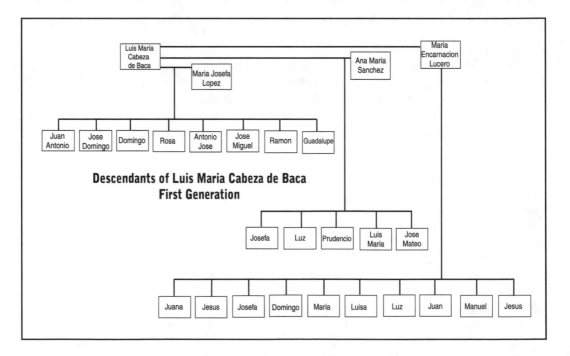

Descendants of Luis Maria Cabeza de Baca
First Generation

from *Los Valles* of the Jemez. Several of the family members relocated to Jemez Springs and ran their grazing operations on the grant from that town. The family also permitted use of their range by herds belonging to members of the Jemez Pueblo. Ethnologist Adolph Bandelier reported seeing *Los Valles* dotted with flocks of sheep in the 1880s.[20]

The Cabeza de Baca family used the traditional community land grant concept to share and utilize the land. Nearly three centuries of Spanish experience with ranching in New Mexico taught herders to share the valuable scare resources of water and grass. Under the community grant system, grantees lived and farmed on their small homesteads near rivers or streams. Community grazing lands were shared by all. For the Cabeza de Baca family, this meant living in Peña Blanca or in the valley of the Jemez River and sharing the grasses of the Valle Grande and other valleys. And with 100,000 acres of property, there was plenty to go around.

Use of the Baca Location No. 1 by the Cabeza de Baca family and their neighbors probably centered not on the Valle Grande but on the smaller *valles* along the north rim of the Valles Caldera. In summer herders set up sheep camps on the Valle Toledo (then called the Valle Santa Rosa), the Valle San Antonio, and the Valle de los Posos. Dates carved on aspen trees still testify to the use of these back valleys as sheep camps before the beginning of the twentieth century. At this time small family groups established summer sheep camps. Utilizing the tall grasses of the valleys, the herders ran small flocks, probably no larger than several hundred animals apiece.[21]

Much of the early sheep herding on the Baca Location No. 1 took place on the Valle Toledo (shown here), Valle San Antonio, and the Valle de los Posos. Several sheep camps on the edge of the Valle Toledo date to the late 1890s.

But the ownership of the Baca Location No. 1 was no simple matter. Luis Maria Cabeza de Baca had 24 children, and by 1860 his descendents included 88 grandchildren and about 60 great-grandchildren. In 1871 John Watts had to track down 86 heirs to purchase the Baca Location No. 5. Shared ownership of the Baca Location No. 1 brought benefits to many family members and many other residents of the region. Only when the concept of shared community resources collided with the American view of property ownership did problems arise.[22]

In 1860 a one-eighteenth undivided interest in the Baca Location No. 1 was assigned to each of Luis Maria Cabeza de Baca's children who survived to adulthood, whether living or dead at that time. The undivided interest in the property gave the grantees the right to share and utilize the water and pasture on the grant, but no attempt was ever made to physically divide the property. As the original heirs died, their interests were divided evenly among their children. For example, Jose Miguel Cabeza de Baca had seven children, each of which inherited one-seventh of Jose Miguel's one-eighteenth undivided interest in the Baca Location No. 1. Each of the children owned an undivided one hundred twenty-sixth interest in the property.[23]

Not all the heirs settled near enough to the Baca Location No. 1 to make it easy to run their stock on the property. This group found little attraction in owning an interest in the Baca Location No. 1 and even before the ink had dried on the final legal papers, some family members sold their interests in the property. With dozens of co-owners and only a vague notion of the legality of owning interests in a large property, other Baca heirs were easy prey for men who thrived on dealing in real estate. Within five years of when the Baca family took possession of their land, three major players emerged as owners of about half of the interests in the property: Francisco Tomas Cabeza de Baca, Santa Fe attorney Thomas B. Catron, and Mariano S. Otero, a real estate speculator from Bernalillo, north of Albuquerque.

Thomas Benton Catron was no stranger to New Mexico land grants. During his lifetime Catron owned outright or held interests in 34 land grants, and during his career as an attorney he represented 63 clients in land grant cases. Catron made his first purchase of a Baca Location No. 1 interest in 1877. Over the next 20 years Catron doggedly tracked down Baca family members and purchased about ten percent of the interests in the grant. One of Catron's purchases was from Teodora Cabeza de Baca, who at the time was living in a mental hospital.[24]

Mariano Sabine Otero was born to a well-to-do Spanish family in the middle Rio Grande valley in 1844. His family included several of the first Hispanic business and political leaders in New Mexico. His uncle, Miguel Antonio Otero, studied law in St. Louis before returning to the newly formed Territory of New Mexico as the private secretary to Governor William Lane. He went on to a successful career in banking and railroads. Miguel's son, Miguel Antonio Otero II, later served two terms as Governor of New Mexico. Mariano put his wealth and connections to good use, dealing in real estate in central New Mexico. He was a powerful force in Bernalillo and Sandoval counties, and served two terms as the New Mexico delegate to Congress. One of Otero's long-term projects was the acquisition of the Baca Location. In 1880 Otero and his uncle purchased the land in the Jemez Valley that included the well-known Jemez Hot Springs. The Oteros energetically promoted building a railroad from Bernalillo up the Jemez River to the springs. Increased visitation to their resort was only one factor in this promotion; undoubtedly they were also eyeing the vast, unexploited timber resources on the Baca Location No. 1. Otero inherited interests in the Baca Location No. 1 from his father-in-law, Jose Leandro Perea, and actively sought out Baca family members to induce them to sell their rights to the property. By 1897, Otero owned about 35 percent of the Baca family interests in the land grant.[25]

The end of the Baca family's ownership in the grant was set in motion with the death of Francisco Tomas Cabeza de Baca. Over the years, through payment for his services during the land grant dispute and through purchasing interests from family members, Tomas had acquired about 20 percent of the total interests in the grant. Francisco's widow, Maria Gertrudis Lucero, was unwilling to continue ownership in the property. She persuaded her children to sell her their interests, and then on August 17, 1881, sold the entire lot of interests to James Greenwood Whitney.[26]

Members of the Whitney family had left New England near the start of the California gold rush. James' brother, Joel Parker Whitney, was quick to size up the situation in Placer County. Rather than invest in gold mines, Whitney started raising cattle, opened a mercantile business, and sold goods to those who sought their fortunes in gold. Before long, Joel Whitney, his brother James, and his father George were among the California upper class. Over the next 50 years, the Whitneys expanded their operations to include mining operations in Colorado and New Mexico and dealing in New Mexico land grants.

Joel Parker Whitney purchased his brother's interests in the Baca Location in 1884, and then set in motion a long-standing deception that has been used for decades to wrest valuable land grants from the original heirs. Rather than share grazing and timber rights with the other owners, Whitney demanded that he receive his legally owned portion of the grant. His suit claimed that he, Catron, Mariano Otero, and dozens of heirs could not reach an agreement on how to divide the land. In 1893 Whitney filed suit against Catron, Otero, and the others, "…that the said real estate be duly partitioned."[27]

At the heart of the partition suit filed by Joel Parker Whitney were the rights to graze livestock in the Valle Grande and the other grassland valleys within the Valles Caldera. Photo by Lawrence Hitchcock, 1921, from the Los Alamos Historical Society Archives.

Mariano S. Otero, Manuel B. Otero, and Miguel A. Otero were first cousins and descendants of Vicente Otero and Gertrudis Chaves. The family settled in Valencia County. In the second generation, Manuel A. Otero ran a merchantile business, Juan Otero made his home in Peralta, and Miguel A. Otero studied law in St. Louis before settling in Las Vegas, New Mexico. Their sons were the major players in the land grant disputes of the 1880s and 1890s.

Whitney's partition suit was not the first time the Whitneys and the Otero family had tangled over real estate. Ten years before, the two families found themselves on opposite sides of a dispute over the Bartolome Baca Land Grant on the Estancia Plain east of the Rio Grande.

Don Bartolome Baca petitioned the Spanish governor of New Mexico, Facundo Melgares, for a land grant of over a million acres and was awarded the grant in 1819. During his tenure as governor of the province of New Mexico under Mexican rule, Baca gave away some of this massive land grant to other colonists. In 1845 Governor Manuel Armijo, gave a land grant of 500,000 acres to Antonio Sandoval that was centered on the original Bartolome Baca Land Grant. Tracking the Bartolome Baca heirs to Mexico City, the brothers Miguel Antonio Otero and Manuel Antonio Otero purchased all the Baca family interests in the Bartolome Baca grant in 1874. Back in New Mexico, Antonio Sandoval deeded his grant to Gervacio Nolan, whose heirs sold the rights to the Antonio Sandoval grant to Joel Parker Whitney in 1881. Both Whitney and the Oteros believed they held legal title to the Bartolome Baca grant.

Manuel B. Otero, who took possession of his father's interests in the grant after Manuel Antonio's death, established a headquarters at Estancia Springs. Prepared to fight the battle in the courts, Otero retained his father's attorney, Thomas B. Catron. Manuel B. Otero also enlisted the services of his cousin, Miguel Antonio Otero II, to help him legally remove James G. Whitney, Joel Whitney's brother, from the Whitney headquarters at Antelope Springs, about six miles north of Estancia. The two families seemed determined to seek a settlement in court.

By August 1883 James Whitney believed the courts were moving too slowly. Later described as "a big blustering fellow, purseproud and egotistical, domineering and ruthless, a man totally devoid of tact...," Whitney made a move. Manuel B. Otero received word from one of his sheepherders that Whitney had forced him out of the headquarters at Estancia Springs and had

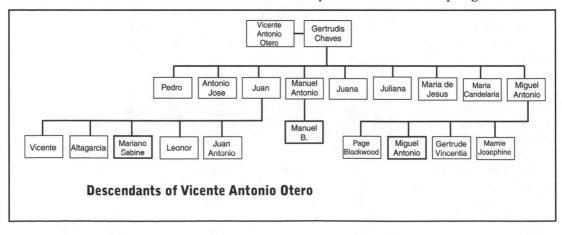

Descendants of Vicente Antonio Otero

taken control of the cabin and springs. Despite the pleading of his family and friends, Otero rounded up several of his men and rode directly to his occupied headquarters. Otero calmly walked into the house and confronted Whitney, asking by what authority the Californian sat at his table. Although witnesses recorded conflicting versions of what came next, the result is clear: inside ten seconds ten shots were fired, Otero and Whitney were badly wounded, and Whitney's brother-in-law was dead. Whitney's version of the story was that he fired in self defense when he saw one of Otero's friends had drawn a gun. The Oteros claimed that Whitney answered Otero's call for authority by reaching for his gun. When the shooting was over, Whitney gasped for his men to surrender. The wounded protagonists were treated by their parties. Otero died by evening, and Whitney's men, fearing they would all be killed by the Otero faction, loaded Whitney on a wagon and started for Santa Fe.

While Whitney as being treated at St. Vincent Hospital in Santa Fe he was served a warrant for his arrest for the murder of Manuel B. Otero. As James Whitney convalesced, Joel Parker Whitney left the east and prepared to remove his brother from Santa Fe. Under darkness, Joel and his workers lowered James from the window of his hospital room, put him on a carriage, and rushed him to the railroad at Lamy where a private car awaited. When the escape was discovered the next morning, the governor of New Mexico was advised of the situation. Governor Sheldon wired the sheriff in San Miguel County and Miguel Antonio Otero II. The two met the train as it stopped for water south of Las Vegas. Otero walked into the Whitneys' car where Joel Whitney attempted to stop him. Otero drew his pistol and put it in Whitney's stomach while the sheriff ordered the railcar hitched to another engine and hauled back to Valencia County. In Albuquerque, Judge Bell stopped the train and ordered James Whitney released on a bond of $25,000. Bell knew a large crowd of Otero supporters awaited the train in Los Lunas, bent on lynching Whitney when he arrived. Whether Bell was acting through a sense of duty or was paid off by Joel Parker Whitney is not known.

James Whitney recovered from his wounds in California, and then returned to New Mexico to stand trial for the murder of Manuel B. Otero. The trial took but one day and on April 29, 1884, Whitney was acquitted of murder. It was believed that Whitney's appearance and pleasant, frank manner led the mostly Anglo jury to rule that Whitney had acted in self-defense.[28]

The web of intrigue surrounding the Whitney partition suit only begins with bad blood between the families. On the surface, the players in 1893 are much the same as those in 1883. Whitney's suit pits him against the Otero family—and Mariano Otero was Manuel B. Otero's first cousin—along with Thomas Catron. However, the threads are tightly interwoven. Whitney's legal

"Because the defendants and your orator can come to no agreement for the due partition of the said 'Baca Heirs Location No. One' and your orator does not know and cannot without the aid of this Court ascertain who are the persons prodeeded against herein as unknown... [he asks] that if it should appear to the Court that an actual partition of the said real estate would be infeasible or unequitable or unduly prejudicial a sale of the said real estate may be ordered and decreed..."

Joel Parker Whitney in his petition to the court for the partition the Baca Location No. 1, 1893.

counsel for the suit was John H. Knabel, a former law partner of Catron. As the case wore on, Knabel was assisted by another former Catron partner, Frank W. Clancy. Clancy defended Catron in a disbarment case that overlapped in time with the Whitney suit.

Whitney claimed that he held the interests to almost half the Baca Location No. 1. The assertion was based not only on the shares purchased by Tomas Cabeza de Baca from other heirs but also on Whitney's belief that the heirs had agreed to pay Tomas one-third of the entire grant. The argument was based on the document signed by the heirs on May 2, 1857 that gave Tomas Power of Attorney to pursue the case.

Catron and Otero immediately started to tear away at the validity of Whitney's claims. Both defendants successfully argued that many of the alleged purchases by Tomas Cabeza de Baca were invalid and that they, either Catron or Otero, held the true interests that were claimed by Whitney. The defendants presented deeds and testimony by family members to support their case. In the Power of Attorney document, the defendants found no statements that promised Tomas one-third of the entire grant. They argued that in the document the heirs agreed only to pay Tomas either in lands or in money, whichever he found satisfactory. No specific amounts were cited or obligations made. In November 1897 Special Master William D. Lee agreed with the defendants, made corrections to the division of interests in the Baca Location No. 1, and struck out Whitney's claim to one-third of the entire grant. With these actions, Whitney interests in the grant dropped to about 20 percent of the total.[29]

The problem of partitioning the grant remained. In October 1898 the court directed a commission to study the feasibility of making a partition of the grant "without manifest prejudice to the owners...." The commissioners visited the property, looked at the division of the 46 valid undivided interests, and ostensibly searched for a way to avoid cheating minority owners.

"Were the four largest individual and family interests the only ones to be considered, a partition could probably be made, that would be just and equitable to each; but, outside of these four individual and family interests, are thirty-four remaining ones...If the location could be partitioned in accordance with the amount of each owner's share, giving him his proper proportion of valley and mountain, it would be impossible to maintain the value of the property as a whole." The commission recommended against an attempt to divide up the property.

The commissioners divided up the nearly 100,000 acres of the property among the interest holders. Joel Parker Whitney was entitled to 19,316.271 acres of the property. Mariano Otero's share amounted to 34,713.633 acres. On the other end of the spectrum, minority owners like Santiago Cabeza de Baca held interest on 112.828 acres. On the surface, the problem was how to award an

"Wherefore this respondent prays that the said report be modified in accordance with the evidence and the facts, and that if it shall appear to the court that any further testimony on behalf of this respondent is necessary that the cause be re-referred for a short time, and he, your respondent, be given an opportunity to supply any missing links of testimony that may be necessary."

Mariano Otero's response to the Whitney suit, 1893.

Parties	Fractional Interest	Allotted Acres	Total Payment
Joel P. Whitney	107/550	19,316.271	$2,966.34
Mariano S. Otero	923/2640	34,713.633	$5,530.86
Pedro Perea	2054/24640	8,276.790	$1,271.04
Josefa Perea de Castillo	689/24640	2,776.390	$426.36
Filomena Perea de Otero	689/24640	2,776.390	$426.36
Beatris Perea de Armijo	689/24640	2,776.390	$426.36
Barbara Perea de Yrisarri	689/24640	2,776.390	$426.36
George W. Harrison	117/24640	471.462	$72.40
Manuela Baca de Perea	131/59136	219.947	$33.78
Lucia Perea de Sowers	131/78848	164.955	$25.33
Lucinda Perea	131/78848	164.955	$25.33
Emiliano Perea	131/78848	164.955	$25.33
Corina Perea	131/78848	164.955	$25.33
Jesus Maria Silva	1/880	112.828	$17.32
Heirs of Isabel Silva de Armijo	1/880	112.828	$17.32
Benito Silva	1/880	112.828	$17.32
Francisco Silva	1/880	112.828	$17.32
David Cabeza de Baca	1/880	112.828	$17.32
Santiago Cabeza de Baca	1/880	112.828	$17.32
Isabel Cabeza de Baca de Sena	1/880	112.828	$17.32
Eulalia Cabeza de Baca de Ortiz	1/880	112.828	$17.32
Jose de Jesus Cabeza de Baca	1/220	451.315	$69.31
Josefa Cabeza de Baca de la O	1/220	451.315	$69.31
Refugia Salazar	1/660	150.438	$23.60
Siria Salazar	1/660	150.438	$23.60
Elsia Salazar	1/660	150.438	$23.60
Antonio Cabeza de Baca	1/140	709.209	$108.01
Felipe Cabeza de Baca de Barryesa	1/140	709.209	$108.91
Jose de Jesus Maria Cabeza de Baca	1/140	709.209	$108.91
Heirs of Jose Manuel Cabeza de Baca	1/140	709.209	$108.91
Diego Cabeza de Baca	1/120	827.410	$127.06
Guadalupe Cabeza de Baca de Leiba	1/120	827.410	$127.06
Francisca Cabeza de Baca de Garcia	1/160	620.558	$95.30
Jose Cabeza de Baca	1/160	620.558	$95.30
Sotero Cabeza de Baca	1/160	620.558	$95.30
Rumualdo Cabeza de Baca	1/160	620.558	$95.30
Petra Cabeza de Baca de Sanchez	1/160	620.558	$95.30
Heirs of Juliana Cabeza de Baca de Sanchez	1/160	620.558	$95.30
Jose Ramirez	1/480	206.832	$31.76
Francisco Ramirez	1/480	206.832	$31.76
Albina Lopez de Ramirez	1/360	275.803	$42.36
Petra Brown de Roival	1/480	206.832	$31.76
Filomena Brown	1/480	206.832	$31.76
Feliciana Brown de Archuleta	1/480	206.832	$31.76
Jesus Maria Brown	1/480	206.832	$31.76
Maria de los Angeles Garcia	1/100	992.892	$152.45
Thomas B. Catron	1151/10080	11,337.494	$1,742.06

The owners of interests in the Baca Location No. 1 with their allotted acres and total payment under the partition sale of March 18, 1899.

owner entitled to 112 acres a piece of land that reflected the value of the property as a whole. The smaller partitions would have to reflect the fraction of the property that was rocky mountain top as well as rich bottomlands. In reality, the inability to equitably divide the land was a frequent ploy to wrest land from the minority owners.[30]

On January 27, 1899, Associate Justice of the Supreme Court of the Territory of New Mexico J. W. Crumpacker ordered that the Baca Location No. 1 be sold at public auction to the highest bidder and the proceeds from the sale be divided among the owners in accordance with their holdings. The sale was made on the steps of the Sandoval County Courthouse in Bernalillo on March 13, 1899. The lands and premises were sold to the highest bidder, Frank W. Clancy, for the sum of $16,548.21.[31]

Five days later, on March 18, 1899, Frank Clancy sold the Baca Location No. 1 to the Valles Land Company. The company had been incorporated on February 20. The owners were Mariano S. Otero and his son, Frederico J. Otero.[32]

The dealings surrounding the partition and sale of the Baca Location No. 1 begs a series of questions. Who was working for whom? What backroom deals were cut in the weeks leading up to the sale, or were the deals in the works from the beginning of the suit? In forming the Valles Land Company, Mariano Otero must have had a plan to acquire the property. Did Clancy outbid him, or had they previously worked out that Clancy would make the purchase and Otero would buy it from him? Whatever the answers, the result was a familiar one. The heirs of Luis Maria Cabeza de Baca no longer held interests in their land grant, which fell into the hands of a single owner.

CHAPTER FIVE
1899 TO 1918

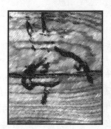

CHANGING HANDS: SULFUR, SHEEP, TIMBER, AND SPECULATION

As the valleys of the Jemez Mountains filled with sheep, the surrounding canyons experienced an influx of development. In the mid-1850s, a settler named Archuleta established crude bathhouses at the hot springs along the lower Jemez River. In 1880 Mariano S. Otero and his uncle Miguel Antonio Otero purchased the bathhouses and developed plans for converting quiet Jemez Springs into a major resort. The next year the investors opened a hotel in town and began a push to bring tourists to the valley. The family ran thriving businesses in Jemez Springs for the next twenty years.

As successful business ventures put more capital in Mariano Otero's hands, he quietly bought interests in the Baca Location No. 1 from family members in Peña Blanca and in the Jemez Canyon. Starting with $200 worth of interests in the Baca Location in 1880, Otero's interests increased to $2,000 in 1892. By 1898

Otero's Baca Location holdings reached $10,246 and he owned 35 percent of the interests in the property.[1]

While increasing his interest in the Baca Location No. 1, Mariano Otero expanded his operations to the thermal waters and minerals available near Sulphur Springs. (According to the 1876 survey of the property, this cluster of thermal vents sat just outside the boundary of the Baca Location No. 1.) Otero was excited about the possibilities of mining sulfur, an idea he probably borrowed from John W. Walton, a miner who had staked out a small mineral claim along the Baca Location's western boundary in 1895. In 1898, Mariano Otero claimed 19 acres adjacent to Walton's claim as mineral property.

Mariano S. Otero came from a prominent New Mexico family and was a successful real estate speculator at the time he completed his purchase of the Baca Location No. 1. Courtesy of the Museum of New Mexico, Negative No. 10327.

"The Sulphurs" is an area of intense thermal activity. The Spanish colonizers of New Mexico knew of these springs along the western edge of the Valles Caldera and named them *Los Azufres*. Amid the conifer forests of a southwest-draining canyon within the western perimeter of the Valles Caldera, Sulphur Hot Springs consists of about ten acres of a bleached and barren landscape. Hot springs, fumaroles, and mud pots dot the valley, and a few springs issue at 190 degrees F. The distinctive feature of the thermal area is the high concentration of sulfur in the water that travels fault pathways in the subsurface to bubble up on the ground. The springs are not so much thermal waters as they are springs that discharge natural sulfuric acid, sometimes with a pH less than 1.[2]

Gases loaded with a high concentration of hydrogen sulfide escaped from the numerous vents and fumaroles on the Otero claim. When exposed to air, rapid cooling of the gases deposited sulfur on the walls of the openings and lined them with brilliant yellow crystals. In 1900 Mariano Otero constructed a small experimental mill at the springs. He extracted enough sulfur from the ore to call the trial a success and then quickly worked to expand the capacity of his digging and milling works.

Otero's immediate need was to haul larger, more productive mill machinery from the railhead at Santa Fe. The speculator took his road needs to the capital in June 1902, agitating for improvements on the road over the Sierra de los Valles from the city to his springs. He argued that a road connecting the two places would bring considerable business to Santa Fe, both from travelers to the resort and from shipments of sulfur from his mines. When the money for the new road proved difficult to raise, Otero made an attractive proposal to the Santa Fe business community. Otero offered to build 13 miles of the road himself, leaving only a two-mile section for Santa Fe businessmen to finance.

By early July Otero had enough subscriptions from Santa Fe to begin construction. By the end of the month, Otero upheld his end of the deal and the road was complete. Using the old military road over Cañon de Valle Pass and several other trail and road segments that were in use, Otero's road skirted the south flank of Cerro del Medio, and headed north into the Valle Jaramillo and the Valle Santa Rosa. Turning west and traveling over low divides in the Valle San Luis and Valle Seco, the road reached the headwaters of Sulphur Creek and easy passage to the mines.[3]

The *Santa Fe Daily New Mexican* was jubilant, saying, "Whole mountains of crude sulphur exist and Mr. Otero has found a good market for it....When milled, the sulphur will be brought to this city and shipped east from here. This will establish quite a freight service between the Sulphurs and this town....And the road will also induce many people to spend their summers at Jemez Springs...."[4]

Otero's heavy mill equipment was shipped by rail to Santa Fe. On August 28 freighter Mert Wagner loaded the machinery on ten wagons and hauled it over the mountains to the mill site. Moving the boiler alone took a team of eight horses pulling and another eight pushing the load. Within weeks ramshackle buildings filled the small mountain valley. The mill was designed to process up to 15 tons of ore per day, and it looked as if there was an endless supply of material to mine. Otero mined some sulfur before snow shut down operations for the year and then restarted in the spring of 1903. At first,

The Otero sulfur mill at Sulphur Springs in 1921. All the milling equipment was hauled by wagon from Santa Fe into the Valles Caldera. Photo by Lawrence Hitchcock from the Los Alamos Historical Society Archives.

digging was easy as much of the mineral was deposited in cracks within a few feet of the surface. But by 1904 mining the sulfur was far more difficult and required tunneling. Operations came to an abrupt halt when it was found that poisonous hydrogen sulfide gas was collecting quickly in the mine shafts. Despite the difficulties, Otero shipped about 200,000 pounds of sulfur out of the Jemez from 1902 to 1904.[5]

At the same time he was developing the sulfur mines, Otero established a hot spring resort on his mining claim. While the mill and mine occupied some of the property, about ten acres were set aside for the development of thermal springs. Otero built crude bathhouses over the largest springs, and in 1902 he added a hotel to the growing resort. Stagecoach service from Jemez Springs to the Sulphurs brought Otero a thin but constant stream of visitors.[6]

After Mariano and Frederico Otero formed the Valles Land Company and purchased the entire Baca Location No. 1, they immediately began livestock operations on the ranch. Although they mostly dealt in real estate, the Oteros were also experienced sheepherders. The partners registered a new brand on June 8, 1899, and brought sheep to the ranch that first summer. On a hunting trip into the Jemez range in November 1902, Coloradoan Harry Sparks rode his horse around the hulk of Redondo Peak, through the Valle Jaramillo, and into the Valle Grande. Sparks wrote in his journal, "There was large numbers of horses scattered over it. Saw a man rounding up horses across the basin [.] it was so far I could hardly make out what he was." In the typical pattern of use, the Oteros grazed cattle and horses on the large *valles* and grazed sheep in the mountains. For lambing grounds the Oteros used the meadows above Sulphur Springs. One benefit of this location was that the herders could use the acidic water from the springs to rid the sheep of scab and ticks.[7]

After Mariano Otero died in a carriage accident in 1904, Frederico Otero and his brothers took over their father's extensive holdings in the Jemez area. Because he was his father's sole partner in the Valles Land Company, Frederico became owner of the Baca Location No. 1. However, what pleasure Frederico derived from the property was short lived. For years Mariano Otero had grazed sheep on the community Cañon de San Diego land grant, correctly claiming his rights as a landowner in Jemez Springs. Over the years Otero purchased a significant portion of the interests in the community grant and by the time of his death had been treating the entire 110,000 acres as personal property. When Frederico and his brothers inherited the interests in the grant, the other owners took the matter to court in an attempt to recover their claim. To settle the dispute, the judge awarded 80 percent of the acres to the heirs of the original grantees and ordered the land grant sold and the money divided. Combined with other losses, the settlement forced the brothers to look elsewhere to add to their cash flow. By 1905 Frederico Otero actively marketed the Baca Location No. 1 to prospective buyers, most of whom hailed from the East Coast.[8]

"All the sulphur at Sulphur Springs was apparently deposited in vents, cracks, and pores within a few feet or a few inches of the surface. ...The deposit occupies a roughly circular area over 600 feet in diameter. Sulphur deposit is not considered commericial. The sulphur is irregularly deposited and is a relatively thin deposit measuring only 2 ft. 4 in. to 3 ft. 4 in. in four cuts in the more promising parts of the area."

Geologist G. R. Mansfield's analysis of Sulphur Springs, 1918

A few of the prospective buyers hired timber cruisers to inspect the Baca Location No. 1, and the cruisers sent glowing reports to the interested parties in the East. One report estimated that over 400 million board feet of "white pine" stood ready for harvest on the property, enough "to keep 6 to 8 mills busy for 35 to 40 years." The report went on to state, "...the country is not so mountainous as others in the region and would be easy to log." Despite the short growing season, the timber cruiser reported that hay, wheat, and potatoes could be grown in the valleys, which were free of stumps and stones. Water and the open valleys filled with grass made the property the best grazing land in the state. Reporting to one of his clients in Chicago, attorney Napoleon Laughlin said he didn't personally know the cruisers who had written the reports, but "if anything, the reports underestimate the value of the property."[9]

Years of financial battles, squabbles with his brothers, and the burden of managing extensive real estate took its toll on Frederico Otero. As he actively pursued the sale of the Baca Location No. 1, Otero sought refuge on the ranch. Frederico Otero would maintain a close tie to the land for the next ten years.

Otero brought his own flocks of sheep and cattle to the Baca Location, but he also made money by leasing summer grazing rights to the fertile *valles*. The timing was perfect for a new private grazing enterprise in the Jemez region. The Jemez Forest Reserve was established in 1905. Suddenly, local herders were forced to pay a fee for using the forest grazing lands on which they had always run their stock. The new fees established by the Forest Service seemed unreasonable, and many refused to participate in the new management system. Otero charged 25 cents per sheep and one dollar per cow for summer grazing rights, and he offered herders the opportunity to avoid dealing with the fledgling Forest Service.[10]

Throughout the summer months, herders from Santa Fe, Española, Cuba, San Ysidro, and Peña Blanca grazed their stock on the lush grasses of *Los Valles*. When biologist Vernon Bailey

Sheep and sheepherders near the Valle Grande, 1921. T. Harmon Parkhurst photo from the Los Alamos Historical Archives.

explored the Jemez Range in 1906, he reported the range conditions in the Valle Toledo to be excellent.[11]

To maintain a close watch of the operations on the ranch, around 1907 Otero established a headquarters on the property. For his headquarters Otero chose a site along the small spring-fed flow of La Jara Creek. On the western edge of the Valle Grande, Otero felled a few trees from a towering stand of orange-barked ponderosa pines to make a two-room log cabin. Smaller logs were placed on a foundation of native stone. Hand-hewn beams supported the steep-pitched roof, a requirement in a place where snow often fell nine months of the year.

A few yards to the north of the cabin, Otero supervised the construction of a log commissary building from which he could sell supplies to the herders using the property. Walls made from peeled ponderosa logs were chinked with mud and straw; crude plank shelving nailed to the logs held the items that were for sale. Water from the creek supplied the compound and was used to irrigate a small field of crops in the Valle Grande just outside the tree line.

Frederico Otero built his headquarters along La Jara Creek. The long cabin to the left in the photograph served as residence and office. Only the middle portion of the modern structure is original. The oldest rooms have a stone foundation and hand-hewn beams. To the right is the commissary building, another log structure made from ponderosa pines that grew nearby.

To connect his properties in the Jemez, Otero built a narrow road from Sulphur Springs to the meadows along Redondo Creek, over a low pass to El Cajete, the "Washtub," and then along South Mountain into the Valle Grande. Connections to the world beyond the mountains were via a rough road to the mining camps in Bland Canyon to the south and a steep road to Española over the pass at the head of Santa Clara Canyon.[12]

Although he lived on the property only during the summer months, Frederico Otero was the first recorded long-term resident of the Baca Location. Otero's selection of the headquarters established the site that remained the center of ranch operations through the time of its purchase for a national preserve in 2000.

New Mexico had long attracted its share of outside capital, usually drawn by the opportunity to exploit the state's natural resources. Grazing and farming were the earliest areas of economic development, followed by extracting minerals from easy-to-dig mines. In the late nineteenth century, as the richest mines played out, investors looked at the untouched forests of northern New Mexico as a way to turn a profit. The situation was no different on the Baca Location No. 1. After only 33 years in the hands of the descendants of the Spanish settlers of New Mexico, the Baca Location No. 1 fell into the hands of Eastern capitalists.

On October 16, 1909, Frederico Otero sold the Baca Location to a Pennsylvania firm, the Redondo Development Company, which was speculating in natural resource development in New Mexico. Two days before the sale Redondo Development filed its Articles of Incorporation with the Territorial Secretary. With one exception, the incorporators were from Pennsylvania; only Willard S. Hopewell hailed from New Mexico. The company had raised $212,000 in capital for the purpose of "colonization, development, etc." of the Baca Location No. 1. Although the Articles of Incorporation mentioned nothing about timber, the investors had their eyes on the ponderosa pines that grew at the foot of the mountain slopes. Redondo Development reportedly paid Otero $300,000 for the property—considerably more than the assessed value of $53,000.[13]

How Redondo Development, which was named for the highest peak on the Baca Location, became aware of such a remote property is not known. Most likely the connection was Willard Hopewell. Born in Chester, England, Hopewell moved to New Mexico after a chance meeting with Miguel Antonio Otero, the great-uncle of Frederico. Hopewell established himself in mining and timber before entering politics and serving in the House of Representatives of the Territory. From 1903 to 1911, Hopewell was manager of the Pennsylvania Development Company, a ranching and coal-mining firm. Perhaps Hopewell's acquaintance with the Otero family and his connection with Pennsylvania investors brought the two parties together in 1909. The company's president, Edward D. Wetmore of Warren, Pennsylvania, described himself as a capitalist in the lumber industry.[14]

The Redondo Development Company hired Lewis D. W. Shelton to survey the property and draw plans to subdivide the land into categories for development. Shelton's map divided the land into a grid of regular numbered sections. The surveyor further delineated prairies for grazing, timber, sites suitable for housing, and "mountains and worthless sections."[15]

The Redondo Development Company's plans for quick development of its land soon came up against the realities of the rigors of the Jemez Mountains. The area remained remote and isolated, linked to the rest of the world only by poor dirt roads. The isolation had not changed much since the 1880s when Adolph Bandelier reported, "...ingress and egress [to the Valles Caldera] are so difficult that even potatoes, which grow there with remarkable facility, can not be cultivated profitably. The descent to the east toward Santa Clara is through a long and rugged gorge. Over a trail which beast or burden must tread with caution, while toward Cochiti the parts are still more difficult. On the west a huge mountain mass, Sierra de la Jara [Redondo Peak] interposes itself...and the traveler is compelled to make long detours in order to reach the Jemez River." The nearest railhead was 30 miles away, and the terrain between was rugged. Transportation costs

"The Valle Santa Rosa [Valle Toledo] is a park like basin about 2 by 4 miles in extent, well watered and covered with luxuriant grasses. A few cattle and sheep do not keep the grass eaten down noticeably and it stands one to 2 feet high, of the best varieties. No one lives in the valley as it is on the Baca grant and is too high for farming."

Vernon Bailey in his field notes, September 5, 1906

would add greatly to construction financing and made the cost of logging prohibitive. At 8,700 feet, winter came early and hard, and the mountain passes were blocked with snow from November to May.[16]

Although the land's worth had always been measured in terms of grazing, Redondo Development had no interest in the livestock industry. While the Redondo directors deliberated on developing and timbering the property, they either never acquired grazing rights or else leased the grazing rights to Frederico Otero. Otero continued to run sheep and cattle on the Baca Location and retained the headquarters area as his summer residence.

Otero's main income continued to be the leasing of grazing rights. The erstwhile owner hired ranch hands to count sheep and cattle as lessees drove them onto the Baca Location in April or May. From May to September, the *valles* filled with about 20,000 sheep and 2,000 to 3,000 cattle. Although overgrazing was already becoming a problem on the surrounding national forest lands, the Baca Location was capable of carrying a far higher capacity.[17]

While Otero used the land for his grazing operations, the Redondo Development Company investigated its new real estate. In the course of Lewis Shelton's mapping of the Baca Location, he found what he

Small-scale logging operations took place near Sulphur Springs as early as 1914. Photo from the Los Alamos Historical Society Archives.

believed to be mistakes in the original survey. Shelton and his crew located many of the original boundary markers, but not as many as he expected. He believed that the original survey of the grant was "partial, incomplete, and wholly and patently erroneous." Most of the error was along the rugged eastern boundary of the property, but also some discrepancy was found along the western boundary. Shelton calculated that the boundaries as surveyed enclosed only 90,425 acres, not the 99,289 called for by the land grant settlement. As a result, the Redondo Development Company felt that it had been unintentionally cheated when it purchased the property.[18]

In July 1910 the Redondo Development Company called for the General Land Office to resurvey the grant and correct the errors. The Surveyor General directed U. S. Surveyor William B. Douglas to investigate. In his report filed in April 1912, Douglas stated that he found many of the original markers along the boundary, but agreed that several were "out of alignment and measure, apparently owing to defective instruments used by the

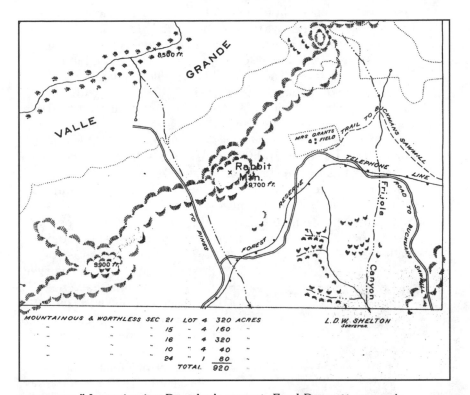

VALLE GRANDE

MRS GRANTS FIELD

TRAIL TO BUCKMANS SAWMILL

TELEPHONE LINE

RESERVE

FOREST

Rabbit Mtn.
9700 ft.

8500 ft.

9900 ft.

TO PINES

Frijole Canyon

ROAD TO BUCKMANS SAWMILL

MOUNTAINOUS & WORTHLESS SEC 21 LOT 4 320 ACRES

"	"	15	" 4	160 "
"	"	16	" 4	320 "
"	"	10	" 4	40 "
"	"	24	" 1	80 "
		TOTAL	920	

L. D. W. SHELTON
SURVEYOR

surveyors." In reviewing Douglas's report, Fred Dennett, commissioner of the General Land Office, dismissed Redondo Development's charges that the survey had not been complete. He believed that a sufficient number of monuments and blazes had been found and confidently stated that the survey had been completed in good faith. Dennett denied the request for a resurvey, stating that since the heirs of Luis Maria Cabeza de Baca had accepted the boundaries as drawn, the property lines would not be corrected.[19]

However, the boundary issue was not closed. Douglas's inspection of the survey line brought to light a discrepancy in the borders of the Santa Clara Pueblo Reservation, the Ramon Vigil Grant, and the Jemez Forest Reserve. The surveyor returned to the Baca Location No. 1 in the summer of 1912 to complete a restorative survey of the boundary. Hiring a crew of three chainmen and three axmen (one of whom died while working on the grueling survey), Douglas carefully set new monuments along the boundary. In the course of redefining the property lines, Douglas determined that the Baca Location as surveyed in 1876 was about 8,000 acres smaller than its legal definition.[20]

Redondo Development officers deliberated over how to regain the disputed acres. In a bold action, they disregarded the lack of a corrected survey and brought in Lewis Shelton to build a fence on the boundary that he believed was the correct line. When the General Land Office learned that the company was

A portion of L. D. W. Shelton's map of the Baca Location No. 1 in 1909. Shelton classified the landscape into timber lands, natural meadows, and "mountainous and worthless sections." Rosa Grant and Ted Mather had a small—and illegal—homestead along the road to Buckman, indicated by Shelton as "Mrs. Grant's Field."

The boundaries of the Baca Location No. 1 were surveyed in 1876, 1911, and 1920. The survey marker at the southeast corner was placed by the 1920 General Land Office. Inscribed inside the right angle is: "BL1/SECOR."

erecting fence on Shelton's line, it filed suit against Redondo Development in an effort to stop the fencing operation. The case was fought through the state district court system for several years before Circuit Judge John C. Pollock ruled in Redondo Development's favor. The General Land Office immediately appealed the decision. On November 18, 1918, the Eighth Circuit Court of Appeals, sitting in St. Paul, Minnesota, affirmed the lower court's decision. The court agreed with Lewis Shelton's assessment that the original survey was never completed. "It is quite apparent that a considerable part of the exterior lines was not traversed at all by the surveyors," Judge Hook wrote in his opinion. "They reported a completion of their work in about one-sixth of the time reasonably necessary for a faithful performance by the force they employed; their contract rate of compensation was by the mile….The case is not one of mere deviation from mathematical accuracy, but one in which a part of what is comprised in the word term 'survey' may be said not to have been performed." Hook went on to instruct the General Land Office to make a correct resurvey of the Baca Location No. 1.[21]

After one final delay, on February 12, 1920, the Surveyor General ordered an independent resurvey of the Baca boundaries. The field portion of the resurvey commenced on June 30, 1920, and carried over into the following summer. Over the year Lawrence A. Osterhoudt, Wendell V. Hall, and Charles Devendorf redrew each of the boundaries of the Baca Location. The surveyors placed brass caps at the corners of the property and erected monuments along the boundary at 1.5-mile intervals. To Redondo Development's satisfaction, the survey returned the missing 8,000 acres to the Baca Location.[22]

However, the redrawn boundary lines created a hardship on one longtime resident of the Jemez range. James Leese and his wife Katie staked out a small homestead in upper Santa Clara Canyon and filed an entry around 1900. Along the road from Española to Jemez Springs, Leese and his wife built a cabin and a barn. Always restless, Leese was constantly on the move. By 1905 Leese had built a second cabin about a mile downstream and, as the local forest ranger, also maintained a residence at the Stone House Ranger Station further east.

Neighbor George White gives a vivid picture of the frontier lifestyle he and Leese shared in 1905. White was employed stringing telephone line in the Jemez when snow disrupted the delivery of his food supply. He and Bill Patterson set off across the Valle Grande to meet the wagons at the Rito del los Indios.

"We got at Rito del Indio and there was no wagons. We didn't have anything to eat, and no beds and the snow was so deep we couldn't get any wood and no horse feed. So we went over the head of Santa Clara about 6 miles. We got at the upper Leese cabin at 2 o'clock in the morning. Hungry and about froze, so we took the horses inside and tore down the toilet to get wood for the fireplace. Could have a fire but no food for us or the horses. We laid down on our saddle blankets in front of the fire and try to rest and sleep. About the time we would get to sleep we would have to turn over and warm the other side so we didn't get much sleep. Next morning we started down the canyon. It was 18 miles to the ranger station and we had to get there before we could get anything to eat. Being about a mile down the canyon there was another Leese house and there was some oat hay in a shed. So we broke it open and fed the horses and we broke in the house and found 2 little old Mexican apples. They were awful good and sweet but small so Bill eat one and I the other. Then we began to ransack for something else to eat. In the bottom of an old barrel we found a pot with some blue sand. So I thought it was Mexican blue corn meal. I told Bill to start a fire and I would go to the creek to get some water and we would have some mush. It turned out to be sand, so we were disappointed - still no chance to eat until after we got to the Station. When we got

James Leese (left) and Macwood Hopper clowning around on the Los Alamos Ranch, circa 1912. Photo from the Los Alamos Historical Society Archives.

there about 4:30 PM, Kate Leese and 3 children were there and all they had to eat was one small can of tomatoes and a small piece of cornbread. So we wouldn't eat it from those children."[23]

George White built his cabin in 1912, but abandoned it shortly thereafter. James Leese filed entry for the homestead in 1915 and built his cabin that summer. Illustration based on the original entry survey map by the U. S. Forest Service.

George White's many years of experience in the Jemez Mountains led him in 1912 to file an entry for a homestead in the Valle de los Posos. White and his wife Lottie built a small cabin in a northern arm of the Posos at the foot of an old trail that crossed the Sierra de los Valles from Guaje Canyon. The western boundary of the 156-acre homestead was drawn along the eastern boundary of the Baca Location No. 1.[24]

Within a year White abandoned his claim. "I gave up because it was too far away from anybody for Lottie to stay with," White said. On June 3, 1915, James Leese filed entry for the former White claim. Three days later the family moved to the Valle de los Posos. The Leese family lived in the White cabin while they built a new two-story log home in a circle of spruce on the west side of the valley. Leese enclosed about three acres of the grasslands with a crude pole fence and planted potatoes and an assortment of

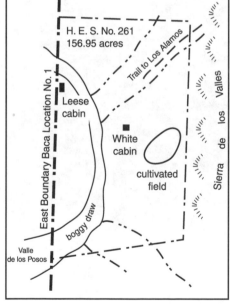

vegetables. When ranger Fred Plomteaux stopped at the homestead in late September, Katie Leese served him dinner in the new house. Plomteaux reported that the house, complete with a corrugated iron roof, was completely furnished and livable. However, Jim Leese was not present because he was working on H. H. Brook's Alamos Ranch.[25]

The Leese family—at least Katie Leese and the three children—occupied the Valle de los Posos homestead for two summers. Jim Leese continued to work at the Brook ranch, but he made frequent trips to the claim. Little was done to improve the land as required by the Homestead Act. The family continued to plant potatoes on three or four acres but did no additional clearing nor did they attempt to irrigate their field, which were required improvements for those seeking to patent a homestead. However, their farming was successful enough for them to grow 15,000 pounds of potatoes in the summer of 1917!

Shelton's 1910 survey of the Baca Location No. 1 suggested that the Leese homestead in the Valle de los Posos sat within the grant boundaries. During the summer of 1918, the family stayed at their home in Española. When the court ruled in Redondo Development's favor in late 1918, Leese was uncertain of the value of continuing to pursue the claim to the homestead. In the following year, Leese filed notice of his intention to make a final claim on the homestead. Ranger Plomteaux was not in favor of granting the

land to Leese. He believed Leese had not farmed the land suffi-
ciently, nor had he made more than a superficial attempt to
occupy the land. Furthermore, Plomteaux accused Leese of
plotting with H. H. Brook to turn the Posos homestead into a small

ranch. The ranger claimed that
Leese would sell the homestead
to Brook as soon as he was
granted the patent.[26]

Leese knew that without a
homestead patent, his claim on
the Valle de los Posos property
was worthless. Without the
support of Plomteaux, Leese
didn't have a chance. Two days
after the boundary resurvey
began, Redondo Development
acquired a quitclaim deed from
Leese. The company paid Leese
for the structures and fencing he
had built on the homestead.[27]

The resurvey also slightly
shifted the southern and western boundaries of the Baca Location
No. 1. As a result, parts of three patented homesteads were found
to be within the boundaries of the property. At the time of patent-
ing, the homesteaders—as well as the General Land Office—
believed their land was outside the boundaries of the Baca
Location. The sulfur mining claims first taken by John Walton and
Mariano Otero were also within the outer boundary of the Baca
Location and legally patented. Because these homesteaders and
miners had received valid title to their land and had acted in good
faith, their ownership was not challenged.

Six years after its acquisition of the property, Redondo
Development had not profited by its purchase. The company
secured a mortgage for $175,000 from the Warren Savings Bank in
Pennsylvania. However, the Redondo Development Company
believed that there was indeed a way to profit from the Baca
Location's timber. In the eight-page mortgage agreement, they
specifically stated that the company retained the rights to do
whatever it pleased with the timber on the property.

*George White and
James Leese
homesteaded in the
upper Valle de los
Posos at the foot of
Cerro Rubio. At
over 9,000 feet, the
valley was not
suited for cultiva-
tion. The ruins of
the two-story Leese
cabin lie in a
clearing in the
surrounding spruce-
fir forest.*

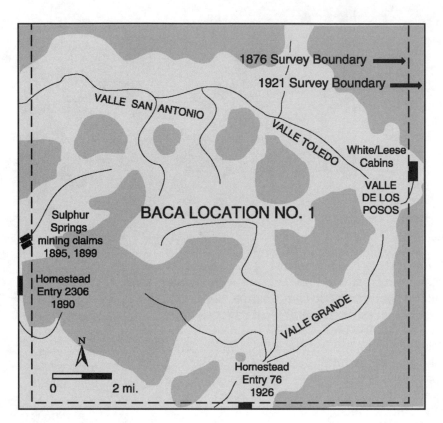

The resurvey of the
Baca Location No. 1
boundary completed
in 1921 affected three
homesteads and two
mining claims. Only
the White/Leese
homestead was not
patented and there-
fore not validated.

CHAPTER SIX
1918 TO 1962

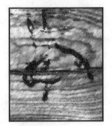

THE BOND FAMILY
IN THE VALLE GRANDE

Sheep were introduced to New Mexico when the first Spanish colonists arrived in 1598, but ranching was difficult in the early days of the colony. Isolated ranches were exposed to the constant threat of attack by nomadic tribes. Tending herds on grazing lands, particularly in the Jemez Mountains, was a dangerous business. However, in colonial New Mexico, a man's influence was determined by the number of sheep he owned. In the Jemez range, herders from the surrounding Spanish ranches and pueblos grazed their sheep in the *valles*, but the lack of artifacts suggests that the number of stock remained low through the late nineteenth century. The increased military presence in the territory starting in 1846, followed by the forced removal of Navajos, Utes, and Apaches to reservations in the 1860s, permitted an increase in livestock grazed in the region. It wasn't until the railroad established a link to outside markets in 1881 that New Mexico saw an explosion of livestock numbers. The wool and mutton industries were the most important economic factor in the territory in the late nineteenth century. By 1890 as many as five million sheep and tens of thousands of cattle were being grazed in the territory. Previously unexploited rangelands were suddenly jammed with stock. For example, from 1885 to 1887 cattle grazing on the Ramon Vigil Grant was at 3,000 head, about ten times the modern capacity.[1]

Frank and George Bond arrived in New Mexico just after the first railroad into the state was completed. Hailing from Quebec, Canada, the brothers tried operating a wool-processing plant in Colorado before opening a mercantile business in Española in 1883. The brothers sold farm goods and brokered in sheep and in wool. Before long, the Bonds controlled a large proportion of the sheep industry in northern New Mexico.[2]

Bond's main sheep and wool company, Bond and Nohl, turned its attention to the rich valleys of the Valles Caldera in 1916 when Bond learned that Frederico Otero would not renew his lease on the property, which would end on April 1, 1917. Although Otero had an option to continue the lease if he specified his desires to the Redondo Development Company before January 1, the former owner had no intention to do so.

In 1917 Frank Bond built this cabin, which faces the Valle Grande, north of the old Otero Headquarters. Photo by Lawrence Hitchcock from the Los Alamos Historical Society Archives.

In November 1916 Bond sent a short, simple note to Edward Wetmore of Redondo Development. "We would be interested in renting the Baca location this coming season. What rental do you ask for it?" Bond wrote.[3]

In December Bond asked Wetmore to write to him immediately after January 1 if Otero did not renew the lease. Having not heard from Wetmore by January 4, 1917, Bond wrote again and impatiently inquired about the status of the ranch. Wetmore replied that the Redondo Development Company would lease the Baca Location No. 1 to Bond and Nohl for $500 per month. The agreement was sent to Bond in February and Bond assumed a five-year lease on the property on April 1, 1917.[4]

Bond hired a few ranch hands and about two dozen sheepherders to work on the property that summer. By early June the property was alive with the Bond sheep herds. In addition to his own stock, Bond followed the business practices of his predecessor, Frederico Otero, and leased grazing rights to other stockowners. Over the next two summers Bond collected grazing fees from $8 to $132 from various lessees.[5]

In addition to beginning his livestock operations on the ranch, Bond was faced with one of the stipulations of the lease agreement. Redondo Development expected Bond to erect fencing around the border of the property. With the ongoing dispute over the grant boundary, Redondo Development wanted to put fence on the Shelton survey line to strengthen its case. As soon as Bond's workers started work on the fence, storms of protest developed from the local pueblos and the surrounding private landowners. Not wanting to alienate his new neighbors, Bond backed off on his promise, and Redondo Development called Lewis Shelton back to the ranch to oversee the fence operation.[6]

After a single season of grazing operations on the Baca Location, Frank Bond could see there was a rich future in operating a sheep empire in the central Jemez Mountains. A two-week long camping trip on the property in the summer of 1917 solidified Bond's viewpoint. In December, Bond incorporated the Quemado Sheep Company for his Baca Location operations.[7]

Despite his agreement only to erect fencing on the Baca Location, in the first year Bond invested $3,054.20 on the property. Included in the first year investments was a cabin along La Jara Creek near the Frederico Otero headquarters. Made of ponderosa logs and native stone, Bond's cabin was built for his daughter Hazel and her husband. Bond hoped to coax his son-in-law into taking an active interest in ranch operations. Hazel's husband never took to the ranch, but the ploy worked on her young adopted son, Gordon McClain. Gordon, who was later adopted by Frank Bond and took his last name, would join his grandfather's business as a young man.

Sheep grazing on the Valle Grande, circa 1920. Photo by T. Harmon Parkhurst from the Los Alamos Historical Society Archives.

On January 21, 1918, Bond wrote a letter to Edward Wetmore of the Redondo Development Company asking him to consider extending his lease on the property for five years. A month later Bond switched tactics and offered to buy the property in four years, at the end of the current lease. Both sides of the proposed sale were experienced and crafty businessmen. Bond said he would buy the property, subject to the resolution of the ongoing litigation in the boundary dispute—thus allowing Wetmore to pay for the attorney fees. Knowing that Redondo was interested in the timber on the property, Bond agreed not to purchase the timber rights, but offered to lease the timber rights to Wetmore for 50 years. Bond suggested that the two parties split the taxes on the property, with the Bond brothers paying the tax on the grazing land and Redondo Development paying taxes on the timber acres. Wetmore's response is not recorded, but it is clear that he made counter offers to Bond's proposals, ones that better suited the lumbering plans of the Redondo Development Company.

Bond hesitated to accept the conditions of sale. His partner, Louis Nohl, had recently died. Frank Bond and his brother George were assuming operations of the Bond and Nohl Company. The Bonds were also in the process of final negotiations with the Pajarito Land Company to purchase the Ramon Vigil Grant just over the Sierra de los Valles from the Baca Location. Citing his concern of making large investments in time of war, on March 20, 1918, Bond withdrew his offer to Wetmore, but ended the letter with "I still want to own the property some day."[8]

The two parties resumed talks in the fall. Both sides were short on cash, and both had every intention of protecting their specific interest in the Baca Location. Perhaps Bond was simply waiting for a resolution to the boundary dispute: within three weeks of the court decision ruling in Redondo Development's favor, the businessmen reached a compromise. On December 17, 1918, the *Santa Fe New Mexican* reported that Frank and George Bond had purchased the Baca Location No. 1 from the Redondo Development Company. A sale contract had been drawn up and signed. Bond agreed to purchase the property, but Redondo Development retained a 99-year lease on the timber of the property, as well as one-half of the mineral rights.[9]

Because Bond already held a five-year lease on the property, the parties agreed to an installment payment plan. The first payment of $50,000 plus interest was to be made by December 31, 1919. Another $50,000 was due two years later, and the balance—for a total of $400,000—was due by the end of 1925. Although the agreement was signed on December 14, 1918, the deed was not executed for six years. In the interim Bond operated the property as his own. Redondo Development had made a profit on the property and still held the rights to the timber.[10]

While negotiations on the sale of the property continued in the summer of 1918, Bond operated seventeen sheep camps on the Baca Location. The camps were scattered from the edges of the Valle Grande to the remote valley of the Rito de los Indios. Teams of herders, the *pastores,* and camp tenders, the *camperos,* watched over flocks of about 1,500 ewes and lambs. *Caporals* used mule trains to keep the camps supplied with what they needed. Most of the employees were of Spanish descent and hailed from the surrounding communities of San Ysidro, Cuba, Española, Peña Blanca, and Vallecitos de los Indios. Two of the Anglo employees were men who knew the area well from years of living in the Jemez Mountains and Pajarito Plateau. Ben White, a restless pioneer who over the years was associated with everything in the region from mining to logging, served as ranch foreman for $125 per month. Wrangler Ted Mather was hired on for $50 per month.[11]

Bond enticed his new son-in-law, Charles Corlett, to serve as ranch manager. Bond built a third cabin at the headquarters area for Corlett and his wife Amy, but that summer the newlyweds were forced to live in a tent nearby as the cabin was built. Corlett served as an officer in Europe during the First World War, but had little experience with ranching. Bond had his long-time associate, John Davenport, oversee ranch operations. Davenport, who was George Bond's nephew by marriage, had managed Bond sheep operations for years and would continue to do so for another two decades. Well over six-feet tall and with a commanding presence, Davenport was soon a well-known fixture in the region. His stature gave him the nickname Juan Largo.[12]

Even after the severe winter of 1918-1919 and the loss of thousands of animals, the Bond sheep empire was developing rapidly. The Baca Location No. 1 was used as summer range; just over the Sierra de los Valles, Bond's winter range was on the Ramon Vigil Grant. Bond used the old military road built to the 1851 hay camp as his stock driveway. Each year, as soon as the pass at the head of Cañon de Valle was free from snow, a constant stream of sheep climbed the canyon-bottom trail from the ponderosa and piñon forests on the Pajarito Plateau to the mountain meadows of the Valles Caldera. The old road remained an important route across the mountains until about 1940.

Despite low pay and often severe working conditions, sheepherders had to carefully manage either their own or their bosses' inventory-on-the-hoof. A single herder might be entrusted

Frank (right) and his son Franklin Bond, Pasadena, California, 1935. Photo courtesy of the Bond family.

with more than $20,000 worth of ewes, lambs, meat, and wool. The job required herders to keep accurate counts of their flocks and to make reports to the owner. Those grazing in remote valleys might not see another human for weeks at a time, and being away from family for five months straight was not an uncommon situation.

A typical sheep camp was carefully located on the sloping sides of small valley meadows, just inside the edge of the forest. Aspen stands were favorite spots, perhaps because the deciduous leaves gave the groves a bright, airy feel. From the camp herders could keep a close watch on the flocks in the grasslands below. Exact locations were selected to provide not only good forage but also bedding areas for ewes and their lambs. Favored spots sat on wind-protected hillsides that offered dry ground, such as the south edge of the Valle Toledo. To ensure a continuous supply of forage, the camps were moved at least once per week. At the end of the season, herders buried all their trash, and burned the pasture areas to encourage next-season grass growth.[13]

For a sheepherder a simple pitched roof tent may have provided shelter, but more often home took the shape of a two-man tepee. The door of the tent faced east or west. In Boy-Scout fashion, herders dug shallow trenches around the shelter to shed runoff during intense storms. In frequently used camps, herders built small rock shelters from the available countryside rock. Firepits could be simple or elaborate and were usually placed six to ten feet from the entrance to the shelter. Food was stored in boxes covered with canvas or in a second tent. Pack stock—saddle horses and horses and mules for packing supplies—was tethered or hobbled nearby; sometimes log corrals were built to hold the animals. Every camp had sheep dogs to help the *pastore* guard and manage the wandering sheep.[14]

Ted Mather leads a pack train across the Valle Toledo. Photo from the Los Alamos Historical Society Archives.

A traditional culture and organization followed the sheep operations onto the Baca Location. Under the long-standing system of sheep operations in New Mexico, the *caporal* supervised a group of three *vaqueros* and nine *pastores*. The *pastores* kept the daily watch over the flocks; *vaqueros* handled the saddle and pack stock. The *caporal* spent most of his time riding to scattered ranges, helping look for lost or stolen sheep, or inspecting the livestock for disease.[15]

Despite camp chores, tending to pack stock, and minding the flocks, sheepherders had many lonely hours on their hands. One universal way to pass some time was to serrate the bark of aspen trees with a knife. The carvings were made with thin-bladed knives; the points gouged through the bark of the aspen and into the soft cambium layer below. As the tree expanded around such a scar, the outer bark turned black, creating a sharp contrast with the milky white bark on the undamaged trunk. The art was often cut at shoulder height, but many carvings stand six to eight feet above the ground.[16]

Several hundred arborglyphs, as they are sometimes called, are found scattered about in the aspen groves of the Baca Location No. 1. As one would expect, the carvings are most common along the edge of the *valles* and adjacent to the sheep trails that traverse the terrain, these being the places where the herders spent the majority of their time. By far the most common carving is a simple inscription of name and date. Universally, the names are Hispanic, such as Alejo Lujan, Alfredo Herrera, and Juan Padilla. Several of the herders left their name in more than one location. Juan Jose Lujan worked on the ranch in 1926 and 1927 and inscribed at least a half-dozen aspens during those years. Known dates of aspen carvings on the Baca Location related to sheep operations range from 1875 to 1962. Other carvings clearly depict memorable events or the dominant thoughts of the herders. Drawings commemorate a favorite dog, a bear sighting, religious symbols, or dreams about the woman left at home.[17]

Unfortunately, many of the carvings are known only from written records or a few photographs. Aspen art is vanishing at an astonishing rate. A major culprit is the expanding elk herd on the property. Elk severely browse the bark from aspens and damage many arborglyphs. In some aspen stands, virtually all the aspens, to a height of six to eight feet, bear scars left by elk. Only the highest or most deeply cut arborglyphs remain visible. Another problem stems from the fact that sheepherders often used the largest aspens to record their passage. Already old trees when the carving was done 80 to 100 years ago, many of the aspens are dead. As the bark peels away from the trunk, the artwork is lost.

Sheepherder Alfredo Herrera carved his name on at least five trees on the Baca Location No. 1 from 1923 to 1948.

Evidence of the long era of sheep-herding takes several faces. Near the Baca Location headquarters is an impressive stand of old-growth ponderosa pine. Some of the massive pines are 400 years old, having their start as seedlings during the earliest years of Spanish occupation of northern New Mexico. The majestic forest set on the edge of the Valle Grande exhibits an unusual set of carvings on four of the oldest trees in the grove. In the early twentieth century, four crosses, each facing one of the cardinal directions, were carved into the pine bark. The grove may have been used as an outdoor place of worship for herders picking up supplies at the nearby commissary.[18]

Life on the Baca Location No. 1, and thus the lives of the sheepherders, was dictated by an annual cycle. The ranch year began in spring on the winter range with the birth of the lambs, but it took some pre-planning to get the timing right. Precious breeding rams, kept year-round in the Bond Company's stable areas along the Rio Grande or on the volcanoes to the west of Albuquerque, were brought to the winter range in November or December. It was a busy time for the rams, whose job it was to impregnate all the ewes in a few weeks. Placing a limit on when the rams and ewes mated gave some control over the timing of the critical lambing period.

Lambing usually occurred in April on the herd's winter range. Now it was the herders' turn to work overtime. The men

Tomeo Chavez, a sheepherder from Cow Springs, New Mexico, camped near Rabbit Mountain in July 1938.

were charged with the care of each mother and newborn lamb. In a flock of 20,000, it was a monstrous chore. Complicating the matter, birthing occurred at all hours and in all kinds of weather. Owners and herders alike dreaded cold snaps or spring snowstorms that could bring disaster to the lambing period.[19]

After the conclusion of the lambing season, flocks were driven to the shearing camps located on the Baca Location No. 1. The earliest corrals for shearing operations were constructed with conifer or aspen logs, but later operations used milled lumber in place of native materials. Frank Bond, and later his son Franklin, placed shearing camps at Paso del Norte Road opposite the road to the headquarters, at San Antonio Springs, and in El Cajete.

Trasquiladores, the wool shearers, came from northern New Mexico, from old Mexico, or in later years from as far away as Australia and the Basque area of Spain. The itinerant workers worked from camp to camp. Usually the work on the first day of shearing camp went slowly as the newly arrived workers recovered from hangovers brought on by their last night in town before heading to the ranch. Using hand shears or later electric ones, the shearers removed the thick winter fleece from the ewes. To prevent time wasted chasing the sheep, shearing was done inside a closed room. To keep track of the number of sheared sheep, one of the Bond workers would hand the *trasquilador* a steel washer, one for each animal completed, to hang on a nail. At the end of the day, the shearer counted the washers and was paid by the fleece, usually receiving 25 cents per animal. A skilled *trasquilador* could shear 50 to 100 sheep per day, but it would take two to three weeks to shear all the animals.[20]

Ranch helpers collected the sheared wool into six-foot-long gunnysacks hung from wooden supports. Small-statured ranch hands climbed into the bags and stomped the wool to compress it and reduce its volume. When filled, each sack held about 500 pounds of wool. The sacks were then rolled to the loading area. From ten to twelve bags were shoved onto horse- or mule-drawn freight wagons. The wool was carted across the Baca Location to the Bond brothers' Española store or through La Cueva to Jemez Springs and on to Albuquerque. Shearing complete, herders and sheep could enjoy the mountain summer.[21]

To turn a profit in the sheep industry, the Bonds not only grazed their own flocks on the Baca Location No. 1 but also engaged in a traditional New Mexico system. For more than a century, the sheep business had depended on the *partido* system. The *partido* system involved the sharing of land and stock between the *ricos* (grant owners) and the herders; it was a way of dividing the profits and the risks of an uncertain business. The system was largely a consequence of the huge land grants in New Mexico. Because the grants deprived small-scale herders of land for grazing, they were forced to turn to grant owners for grazing lands.[22]

Browsing elk have damaged many of the aspen carvings on the Baca Location No. 1.

Many variations of the *partido* system could be found, but the basic operation was always the same. Under contract the *partidario* received a small herd of sheep from the *patron* as a seed flock. The *pastore* drove the flock to the mountains for the summer, fattening them on the alpine grasses and caring for newborn lambs. After a specified period of time, the *partidario* returned the original number of sheep to the *patron*. As fee for use of the sheep, the *partidario* gave a percentage of the sheep born into the flock since the contract began, as well as a percentage of the wool produced by the sheep. Usually it was the responsibility of the *partidario* to compensate for all losses incurred during the time period. Some contracts stated that in five years, the *patron* had to be repaid the number of original sheep, thereby doubling his flock. It added up to an easy way for the *patron* to increase the number of his sheep while the risks were borne by the *pastore*.

Contracts between the *patron* and *pastore* were standardized by an extensive history. The contracts between Bond and his herders were similar to one signed by Jose M. Antonio Montoya in 1829:

Aspen groves were the preferred campsites for sheepherders on the Bond Ranch.

"I the citizen Jose Antonio Montoya, resident of Corales, in the presence of two witnesses, by this declare that I have received from Don Vincente Armijo, a resident of Albuquerque, to my entire satisfaction and contentment, one thousand five hundred ewes on shares. According to the usual custom twenty per cent of the sheep and wool are to be paid as interest since the twenty-ninth of August of the past year of 1829 when I received the fifteen hundred ewes, of which I have possession until April of 1831, three hundred rams and as many bundles of wool since the time when the agreement was made, giving each year the total income or share of the whole quantity. For the assurance of the said ewes and their progeny I obligate my person and property that I have and may have, notwithstanding irreparable accidents such as the invasion of enemies, death by lightning bolts and common loss of which perils, should they happen to me, I shall give immediate notice to the nearest Judge and, in order that I may be believed, shall submit myself to the National Lord Judges. In order that they with all vigor may legally compel me to keep this obligation, renouncing the said mandatory allegation which was and shall be of the terms and conditions aforesaid. In virtue of which, for this contract, I authorize this document that, although it is judicial, I wish to have the same force and validity as if it were made before a competent judge and on the sealed paper as it ought to be. Because there was none it was made (as it is) for lack of which I promise to make a new one when opportunity comes with all proper formalities, notwithstanding the obstacles that have hampered me now."[23]

Like other merchants dealing in the sheep industry, Bond instituted a variation of the *partido* system. His merchantile company sold goods to the herders on credit that could be paid off by caring for company sheep. At the end of the season, the herder's account was credited in the amount of increase in sheep and in the weight of wool brought back to the company store. With the credit and a bit of luck, in a few years a *partidario* might set himself up with an adequate-sized flock, but often that was not the case. Within five years many *partidarios* owed the company a substantial debt. Cold weather, drought, predators, and the rigors of the range all conspired against the small-scale herder.[24]

Under Bond's *partido*, a herder leased a specified number of ewes for three to five years. Rent was to be paid in wool and lambs, usually 300 pounds of wool and 25 lambs per 100 ewes. Any stock the *partidario* owned served as collateral. For grazing on the Baca Location, even if caring for Bond's sheep, the *partidario* was charged a grazing fee. With supplies coming from the company store, Bond often made a hefty profit on all the grazing on his property.[25]

Throughout the 1920s and 1930s, Bond's sheep ruled on the Baca Location No. 1. In 1930 the Bond company established a national record by placing 30,000 sheep on Eastern markets in one day. That year 140,000 sheep grazed on Bond ranches in northern New Mexico and almost 10 million pounds of wool were produced. Despite his hard-nosed attitude toward business, Frank Bond found pleasure in owning the Baca Location beyond its profitability. Bond loved to fish, and from 1917 until he was no longer able to make the journey, he spent two weeks a year in the central Jemez Mountains, trying his luck on the streams.[26]

Since his arrival in the state in the 1880s, Bond had maintained his business headquarters and residence in Española. In 1925, he moved his family to Albuquerque in hopes of improving their health. Shortly after his move, Bond reorganized his business interests and formed Frank Bond and Son, Ltd. The shift placed more responsibilities on Bond's son, Franklin. Former Baca Location manager John Davenport supervised all the Bond interests in northern New Mexico, including the oversight of the former land grant. During his first years in Albuquerque, Bond was hit hard by the deaths of his parents, his wife, and two daughters. Frank Bond moved to California and Franklin took over direct control of the company, but made frequent trips to the West Coast to visit and consult with his father.[27]

Franklin Bond ran the family businesses from Albuquerque, but during the summer he spent many weekends on the ranch with his family. Bond always wore a tie, even when riding on the ranch. Photo courtesy of the Bond family.

Franklin Bond gave the family's ranch operations a more modern outlook. After selling their winter range on the Ramon Vigil Grant to the Soil Conservation Service in 1937, the Bonds acquired the Volcano and Alamo Ranches on the mesas west of the Rio Grande near Albuquerque. Cattle became more of a part of the Baca Location No. 1 grazing program than in the past. With his father's keen eye for business, Franklin said that sheep and cattle prices seemed to balance out: when one was high, the other was low. Each fall Bond sheepherders drove the sheep south along San Juan Mesa and through the village of Ponderosa to the grasslands on the plains northwest of Albuquerque. Breed-stock cattle were driven over the road to Bland, then across the southern Jemez Mountains to Ponderosa, then south to the winter range.[28]

During their ownership of the property, the Bonds permitted the people of the surrounding pueblos various types of access to the property. Through the 1940s, Jemez people received permission to conduct ceremonies on the property. Limited hunting was also allowed, and perhaps included the construction of traditional log hunting structures. However, the Bonds put restrictions on grazing at a far earlier date. At first the Bonds continued the practice of the previous owners of the Baca Location No. 1 by allowing the residents of Jemez Pueblo to graze limited numbers of horses, sheep, and cattle on the ranch. Around 1920 a misunderstanding between the owner and the Jemez Pueblo resulted in the arrest of three Jemez families for illegal grazing. Shortly after the case went to court, permission for pueblo members to graze on the ranch was denied.[29]

The Bonds were good neighbors to A. J. Connell, the director of the Los Alamos Ranch School founded in 1917. Throughout their ownership the Bonds generously permitted the students at the school to camp, hunt, and fish on the Baca Location. Ted Mather, who had worked for Frank Bond during the rancher's first year of leasing the property, was the head wrangler at the school and had an intimate knowledge of the Baca Location No. 1. Many of the boys, who mostly hailed from eastern cities, caught their first trout in the East Fork of the Jemez in the Valle Grande. Each year the school ran a summer camp that included a three-week trail ride through the Jemez. The route generally started at Camp May in the Sierra de los Valles above the school and descended a steep trail into the Valle de los Posos.

Franklin and Mary Ann Bond picnicking on the Valle Grande. Photo courtesy of the Bond family.

A camp was set up along the Rito de los Indios, and the route to the San Pedro Parks passed through the Valle San Antonio.[30]

During World War II the demand for wool was greater than ever. At the time almost all military uniforms were made from wool. Bond sheep continued to dominate the supply of wool produced in New Mexico. Just weeks before the war ended, Frank Bond died in California on June 21, 1945. His death was a parallel to the fate of the sheep industry: as war-developed synthetics found their way into commercial uses, the demand for wool dropped dramatically.

Franklin Bond continued to run sheep on the ranch, but cattle became increasingly important. In the 1950s as many as 12,000 head of cattle grazed on the *valles*. Much of the operation of the ranch switched from *partidarios* to hired cowboys to tend the stock. The Bond ranch employed between five and fifteen cowboys in the summer. The ranch hands would be up at 4 AM for a hearty breakfast and arrive at the corrals at 5 AM. Out of the herd of 50, each cowboy was assigned six or seven horses— enough for a week of hard riding. On the trail by sunup, the employees rode up to 20 miles a day, checking on the cows and calves, inspecting watering holes, and tending other ranch chores. Branding operations were run at Black Corrals near Cerro La Jara in the Valle Grande. During branding time cowboys rode out before sunrise to round up cattle. By afternoon they returned with the stock, the fires were hot, and the branding began. In the 1940s and early 1950s, cowboys and sheepherders received $90 per month. Skilled horse trainers could make $125 per month. Meals were served at the bunk-house and consisted of lamb, beef, potatoes, chili, and fresh pie twice a day.[31]

To supervise the ranch work, Bond hired local young men just back from serving in the war. Richard Boyd took over the ranch's cattle operations and worked closely with John Davenport out of the ranch headquarters. To post a hired hand near the cattle pastures on the Rio San Antonio, Bond built a cabin near the hot springs in the Valle San Antonio. Richard Fitzgerald and his wife Jesse Fenton Fitzgerald moved into the log structure, and long-time wrangler Ted Mather bunked in the "sleeping shack" a few yards away, taking his meals with the Fitzgeralds. Sam Hill came to the ranch to manage the sheep operations. Bond built another cabin in the

Until trucks made the move easier, cattle were herded between the winter and summer ranges on stock trails. Jim Ditto took this photo of the last cattle drive in 1948. From the Los Alamos Historical Society Archives.

headquarters area for Hill and his wife Bertilla. Because Bertilla had a reputation for being wild on occasion, the Hills' cabin was located almost a quarter mile south of the other cabins in the headquarters area. For cowboys working the Valle Grande, the old cabin built by Frederico Otero served as a small bunkhouse. A pot of beans and a pot of coffee always simmered over the wood fire in the bunkhouse.[32]

The years during and after the war were the high point of life on the ranch—which they simply called the Valle Grande—for the Bond family. Franklin's wife Ethel and their children—Amy, Mary Ann, and Frank—spent summers on the ranch, where they lived in the original Bond cabin at the headquarters. Horseback rides and picnics were a part of almost every day. Young Frank helped with ranch chores whenever his young years measured up to the task, which they frequently did. Ethel entertained guests at the headquarters, including Robert and Kitty Oppenheimer on Sunday escapes from the demands of the Manhattan Project. Despite an enlarged heart due to rheumatic fever, Franklin Bond tried to spend weekends on the ranch. Forever the businessman, he always wore a white shirt, tie, and crumpled Stetson hat, even when riding horses or going fishing. As more staff came to live on the ranch, Ethel Bond wanted another cabin for the family. She selected a site on a knoll a few hundred yards north of the other buildings in the headquarters area. A foundation was poured, but the project was never completed.[33]

Shortly after the war, it became more efficient to truck cattle to and from the *valles* from their winter ranges, and the last cattle drive over the Sierra de los Valles took place in 1948. Sheep operations continued on the ranch even as the number of cattle

The Bonds built the San Antonio Cabin in about 1947 to allow ranch hand Richard Fitzgerald and his wife to stay in the Valle San Antonio where the cattle grazed. Building this and other cabins on the property was part of the modernization from sheep to cattle operations.

increased. Cows and calves stayed in the *valles*, and the sheep grazed in the high country. In the later years, herders received assigned locations for their stock and were forced to move camp more frequently than the traditional once per week. As local herders dropped out of the operation to take higher paying jobs in the city, the Bonds hired Basque sheepherders for two or three year stints.[34]

In 1949 Franklin Bond faced a problem brought on by his new eastern neighbor, the community of Los Alamos. During a cold snap in the winter of 1947-1948, the gas pipeline from Santa Fe to Los Alamos failed. The Atomic Energy Commission (AEC) worked with the Zia Company to plan a new pipeline to bring in gas from Farmington. The shortest route cut straight across the central Jemez Mountains. Bond and the AEC negotiated an easement to locate a portion of the pipeline in the northern *valles* of Baca Location. The pipeline entered the property at Twin Cabins Canyon on the western boundary, descended into the Valle San Antonio, paralleled San Antonio Creek into the Valle Toledo and Valle de los Posos, then climbed the eastern rim of the caldera on its way to Los Alamos. For construction and maintenance, the AEC added a road parallel to the pipeline for its entire length.

During these years Franklin's son Frank Bond spent every summer on the ranch. He rode with the other ranch hands, frequently spending all day in the saddle. To insure an even use of the range, the cowboys moved the cattle from place to place, even within the larger valley. In the early 1950s, the family grazed about 5,000 cattle and as many as 30,000 sheep on the ranch.[35]

Franklin Bond died in 1954 at the age of 52. Around the same time John Davenport retired, and Gordon Bond, the adopted son of Frank Bond, assumed the role of ranch overseer. Gordon had little experience with day-to-day ranch operations, but he continued Franklin's attempts to modernize the ranch. Ethel Bond remarried and she and her new husband, Oscar Huffman, had little interest in the ranch. Daughter Mary Ann and her husband Dan Bunten lived and worked on the ranch, holding a continued interest in the property. But by 1957 it was increasingly difficult for the family to operate the ranch. The Baca Location No. 1, and other family holdings, were placed in the Bond Estate Trust.[36]

In 1959 the Bond Estate leased the property to the King Brothers of Stanley, New Mexico. Sam King and his brother Bruce—who would later serve three terms as the governor of the state—signed a five-year lease on the property. The Kings helped move the last of the Bond sheep off the Baca Location. The passage of the last sheepherders is recorded on the door of the old Bond Commissary. As they stopped in for supplies at the outpost, herders from Española, Dixon, Cañoncito, and other towns penciled their names and dates on the commissary door.

The King brothers settled in to run cattle on the ranch. Ranching in 1960 was a far cry from the first days of Frank Bond on the Baca Location. Cows and calves were trucked to the summer range when the *valles* cleared of snow in May. The King operations grazed 3,100 head that year. Starting in mid-September, cowboys rode out each morning to round up the cattle spread over extensive rangeland. It took two weeks to herd the cows and

Franklin Bond and his daughter Mary Ann on the porch of the "Little Cabin," which was originally built for Franklin's sister Amy in 1918. Photo courtesy of the Bond family.

calves into the large pastures of the Valle Grande. In early October heifers were cut from the herds and moved to the loading pens at the old Bond shearing camp near the headquarters road. Seven trucks, all loaded in two hours, took the yearlings to market in Denver. The Kings trucked the calves to feedlots near their home ranch in Stanley, and kept the cattle on the Alamo Ranch near Albuquerque, which they had purchased from the Bonds for winter range.[37]

Like many ranchers before them, the King Brothers were impressed with the grazing potential of the Baca Location No. 1. Knowing that the Bond family was interested in selling the property, they tried to scrape up enough cash to buy the ranch. However, their recent purchase of the Alamo Ranch left them stretched to the limit. They offered to purchase 25,000 acres of the ranch, but the Bond Estate refused to divide the property.[38]

Sheep grazed on the Baca Location No. 1 for more than 75 years, and the lingering effects of the over 250 years of continuous use by sheep and cattle are visible throughout the property and the Jemez Mountains. The species composition of the grasslands was altered as preferred grasses were consumed and unpalatable species flourished. Importation of livestock also brought alien species such as dandelions, Kentucky bluegrass, and red clover to the grasslands. Most importantly, as sheep consumed grasses down to the roots, they changed the role of fire in the Jemez ecosystem.[39]

The upper right corner of the photo shows the meadow on the south face of Pajarito Mountain, circa 1963. Tree invasion into the montane grasslands was just beginning. Photo from the Los Alamos Historical Society Archives.

Evidence from tree rings demonstrates that before 1880, low intensity surface fires swept through the grasslands and ponderosa pine forests throughout the Jemez Mountains. Ignited by high-frequency lightning strikes, mostly during the dry, windy New Mexican spring, these fires were carried along the ground by tall grasses. The flames rarely reached into the crowns of the pines, and the thick-barked old trees were fire-resistant. The fires served to kill off many young conifers and aspens that sprouted in the grasslands. The ground fires maintained the grasslands and the open nature of the ponderosa forests, where between fifty and a hundred trees stood on an acre.

Intense sheep grazing eliminated the grassy fuels. Lightning striking a tree likely burned only that tree without spreading. Any larger fire that did ignite fell under the jurisdiction of the U. S. Forest Service, which had a policy of suppressing all fires as quickly as possible. Without frequent low-intensity fire, small trees growing in the grasslands or ponderosa stands matured. Aspens and conifers encroached into the south-facing meadows on many Jemez peaks, closing in the grasslands that had been there since the retreat of the Ice Age. In the ponderosa stands, thickets of small-diameter pines choked the forest, increasing the number of trees per acre to the thousands. When an ignition occurs in such conditions, the dense fuels create a laddering effect, funneling fire to burn into the tree crowns, and often thousands of acres of forest are reduced to areas of thin soil and standing, blackened sticks.

A flock of sheep in a small mountain meadow near Redondo Peak, 1921. Note the tall grasses growing in the meadow. Photo by Lawrence Hitchcock from the Los Alamos Historical Society Archives.

Tree encroachment into meadows at the head of Cañon de Valle on the south face of Pajarito Mountain. The top photograph, taken in 1935, shows extensive meadows on the flanks of Pajarito Mountain. A few small aspen stands grow in the grasslands. The bottom photograph, taken in 2001, shows a shrinking meadow as trees encroach from all sides. Aspen, spruce, and fir dot almost the entire meadow area. Photos by the United States Geological Survey.

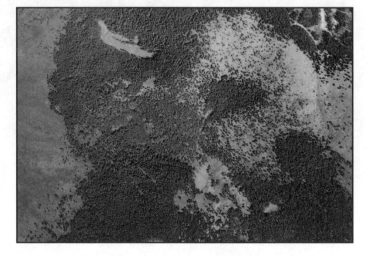

CHAPTER SEVEN
1962 TO 1964

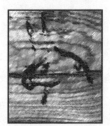

PAT DUNIGAN AND THE BACA LAND AND CATTLE COMPANY

In the early 1960s public awareness of the Valles Caldera grew to an unprecedented high. Clarence Ross and Robert Smith published their landmark work on the geology of the caldera. Throughout the United States the growing environmental movement brought large parcels of relatively untouched roadless areas to the attention of preservationists. The concept of wilderness and of protecting natural landscapes for their own sake turned the eyes of many to the Baca Location. But the idea of preserving the Valles Caldera as public land was nothing new. Even in 1960, interest in including the Valle Grande and its surrounding mountains within federal land management had a long history.

Proposals to create a national park on the Pajarito Plateau dated back more than 70 years. The first suggestion for a national park on the Pajarito Plateau was set forth in 1888 when, due to the writings of ethnologist Adolph Bandelier and journalist Charles

*A. J. Connell,
director of the Los
Alamos Ranch
School, was among
the staunch oppo-
nents of Edgar Lee
Hewitt's Cliff Cities
National Park plan.
Students from his
school frequently
used the Baca
Location No. 1 for
their pack trips.
Photo from the Los
Alamos Historical
Society Archives.*

Lummis, Indiana congressman William S. Homan introduced a bill to protect archeological sites northwest of Santa Fe. In 1900 archeologist Edgar Lee Hewitt took up the cause. Seeking a way to protect the ruins and artifacts scattered by the thousands across the flanks of the Jemez Mountains, Hewitt lobbied Congress to create Pajarito National Park. Lack of interest on the federal level killed the first attempt, but the persistent Hewitt continually pushed his proposal in Congress for more than two decades. At least seven bills to establish a park were introduced in Congress between 1900 and 1919, each with new components that attempted to accommodate the concerns of nearby pueblo members, cattlemen, loggers, and homesteaders. Opposition by the local population played a large role in the defeat of every Pajarito park bill introduced in Washington. A compromise was reached in 1918 with the establishment of Bandelier National Monument.[1]

In 1923 Hewitt tried again. Sensing that it was his last opportunity to steer a park bill through Washington, Hewitt's idea took yet another new twist. The archeologist expanded the scope of his proposed park to encompass the complete range of natural features in the Jemez, including the Valle Grande and the entire Valles Caldera, into a Cliff Cities National Park. The National Park Service (NPS) recognized the merit of Hewitt's latest idea and requested the expansion of Bandelier National Monument. The NPS wanted their park to encompass the pueblo ruins of Puye and Otowi, and included a transfer of 195,000 acres from the U.S. Forest Service to the new park.

From the start, the proposed park faced obstacles that would prove impossible to overcome. Much of the land within the park's boundaries was in private hands. Frank Bond, owner of the Baca Location No. 1, had invested years and a considerable sum of money on the Baca Location. Bond wanted no restrictions on his sheep operation in the Valles Caldera and he was outspoken in his opposition to the new park. To the east, A. J. Connell, the director of the Los Alamos Ranch School, vehemently opposed the park idea. More importantly, the Forest Service opposed the removal of so much land from the realm of economic development that the agency worked to foster. After two years of rallies, meetings, and arguments, the park plan was abandoned.[2]

Twenty-five years of failure in the effort to create a national park on the Pajarito Plateau beyond Bandelier National Monument convinced the NPS that a park based primarily on the archeological attractions of the area wouldn't work. In the late 1930s, the NPS shifted its attention to the geology of the Jemez Mountains and laid the groundwork for a new park centered on the Valles Caldera. In 1938 H. E. Rothrock of the Naturalist Division of the Park Service, with concurrence from the United States Geological Survey, recommended that the NPS establish a national park in the Jemez Mountains.

Rothrock's proposal, which he called the Jemez Crater National Park, placed geology, not cultural resources, as its centerpiece. Compared to previous proposals, the new plan encompassed a vastly expanded area of over a million acres, which was four times larger than any of the plans from the 1920s. The park would include the entire Valles Caldera, and thus all of the Baca Location No. 1, the ancient pueblo villages on the mesas to the north and south, the Bond-owned Ramon Vigil Grant on the Pajarito Plateau, and the Cañada de Cochiti Grant.

It was a grandiose scheme with a fatal flaw: only a small portion of the land in Rothrock's park proposal could be acquired without the approval of the current landholder. Half of the property was in private hands and would require wrestling sales agreements from the owners. The other 500,000 acres would have to be transferred from the Santa Fe National Forest, which had no interest in adding any of its land to the park system. Despite intense lobbying from Rothrock, the proposal never left the Department of the Interior.[3]

Students from the Los Alamos Ranch School take a rest stop on the Baca Location No. 1 in the 1930s. Photo from the Los Alamos Historical Society Archives.

For the next 20 years, neither the public nor the federal land management agencies pushed for government acquisition of the Baca Location No. 1 and the idea seemed not merely quiescient but stone cold. Starting in 1946, the Atomic Energy Commission (AEC) ruled Los Alamos on the eastern border of the Baca Location and functioned as a third powerful federal landowner in the region. The AEC, driven by a need for security, opposed any shift to public ownership of the adjacent block of land. But in 1961 a long-time resident of the Pajarito Plateau initiated another sequence of events that again moved the nation to consider the creation of a park in the Valles Caldera.

Evelyn Frey moved to Frijoles Canyon in 1925 to operate the concession for guest services at Bandelier National Monument. A strong, independent woman, Frey loved the Jemez Mountains and was a friend to all her neighbors, including the Bond family. Indeed, everyone in northern New Mexico seemed to know Frey, and her connections stretched far beyond the canyon walls. On February 26, 1961, Frey wrote a short letter to New Mexico Senator Dennis Chavez, informing him that the Baca Location No. 1 would be put up for sale. Frey suggested that the federal government investigate the possibility of purchasing the property. Chavez contacted the National Park Service, which immediately expressed interest in acquiring the Valle Grande and the encircling mountains.[4]

The Bond family found it increasingly difficult to turn a profit on ranching in the caldera and the Bond Estate did not wish to take on the massive task of running the sheep and cattle operations. The rising cost of hauling cattle in and out was another important consideration. In the late 1950s the estate signed a four-year lease on the land with the King Brothers of Stanley, New Mexico, ending the Bond family's direct management of the property.[5]

Word of the possible availability of the property spread throughout the region. On April 10, 1961, an editorial in the *Santa Fe New Mexican* suggested a park that included the Valle Grande. Los Alamos resident John V. Young, a longtime supporter of outdoor recreation, pushed for immediate action. "It would indeed be a shame if we were to wait until the Valle Grande is cut up for summer cabin sites or becomes a private golf course for a Texas oil baron," Young wrote.[6]

In early May Bond trustee William Sganzini wrote to New Mexico Senator Clinton P. Anderson to inform him of the family's willingness to discuss selling the Baca Location No. 1 to the government. Anderson knew of the opportunity from his colleague Senator Chavez, and as a longtime champion of conservation, Anderson relished the idea of creating a national park in his home state. The senator pursued the idea of public ownership of the Baca Location for its excellent recreational potential and the chance to preserve such an extensive tract of land. He saw economic benefits, too, and estimated that a northern New Mexico national park would pump an additional $100 million per year into the state's economy.[7]

Sganzini spoke to Anderson about the family's wish that the property be converted into a national park. But when Anderson talked purchase price with the Bond Estate, the two parties didn't see eye to eye. The senator believed that grazing land above 8,500 feet was only of marginal quality for cattle and suggested that the price for the entire tract was less than $2 million. The Bond Estate violently disagreed. Not only did the Bonds have years of experience with cattle on the property, but they also believed they could sell small parcels of the property to a significant number of buyers and make as much as $50 million.[8]

While Anderson negotiated with Sganzini, the National Park Service dusted off its plans for the Jemez Crater National Park and again focused on featuring the geological significance of the Valles Caldera. At the time it was widely believed that the caldera was the world's largest volcanic crater and the Park Service envisioned the area as a high-quality attraction. Combined with the extensive archeology of the pueblos in Frijoles Canyon, the explosive story of the caldera would create a park of national significance.

Not everyone was pleased with the possibility of a national park on the Baca Location. As word of the possible sale leaked to the public, sportsmen were vocal in their opposition. The New Mexico Department of Game and Fish, the local Izaak Walton League, and other groups supported acquisition of the property, but wanted it to be managed by the Forest Service, thus allowing hunting and fishing. Thomas P. Gallagher of New Mexico Timber also opposed the park plan. Gallagher owned the timber rights to the property (see Chapter Eight) and was developing plans to cut trees bordering the Valle Grande and to build sawmills on the site. "The government would find itself in a rather strange position if they bought only the Valle Grande meadow, and found us later operating portable sawmills, spewing slabs and sawdust across the national park," Gallagher wrote to Anderson.[9]

After a year of talks with little progress, the Bond trustees told Anderson they were seeking a commercial buyer for the property. Having invested considerable energy into trying to work a deal, Senator Anderson wasn't willing to give up. He convinced the trustees that he could quickly secure funding and steer the park proposal through Washington. When the Bond trustees agreed to wait and see what happened over the next few months, Anderson introduced a bill to establish a Valle Grande National Park on May 17, 1962. The senator had the unfailing support of Secretary of the Interior Stewart Udall. The NPS realized that, even with Anderson's and Udall's

The 1962 park proposal did not include many of the significant features of the Valles Caldera within the boundaries. El Cajete, the oval valley shown here, and the Banco Bonito flow were not included in the proposal. Photo by the United States Geological Survey.

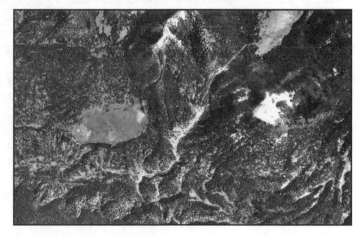

backing, the magnitude of the 1938 proposal would have to be scaled back to suit the existing political climate. Even so, in addition to the purchase of the Baca Location No. 1, the initial proposal for the new park included 67,500 acres of Forest Service land. Anderson and Udall anticipated and received stiff opposition from the Forest Service. In an attempt to reach a compromise NPS and Forest Service officials met in August 1962, but without success.[10]

After a tour of the Bond property two months later, Stewart Udall developed a solution acceptable to both agencies. The secretary suggested that only the Valle Grande become part of the new national park and the remainder of the Baca Location fall under the jurisdiction of the Forest Service. The Valle Grande's 30,649 acres would be attached to Bandelier National Monument through a corridor transferred from the Atomic Energy Commission and the area would be renamed Valle Grande National Park. Udall's compromise successfully broke the impasse between the agencies, and the plan met with approval at public hearings in Santa Fe. Anderson introduced a new bill in Congress on January 9, 1963, and the chances for passage looked good.[11]

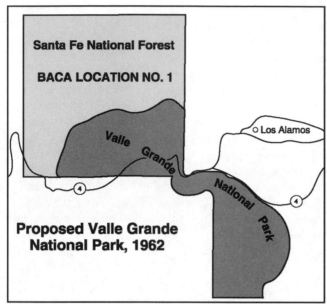

Santa Fe National Forest

BACA LOCATION NO. 1

Valle Grande

○ Los Alamos

National Park

Proposed Valle Grande National Park, 1962

Secretary of the Interior Stewart Udall worked a compromise between the Forest Service and the NPS that would have given the bulk of the Baca Location No. 1 to the Santa Fe National Forest, and combined the area of the Valle Grande with Bandelier National Monument to create a new national park.

Unbeknownst to Senator Anderson or the agencies, the rug had been pulled from under the laboriously derived compromise. On January 29, the *Santa Fe New Mexican* announced with bold headlines that a Texas group of investors had purchased the Baca Location from the Bonds. John Young's Texas oil baron had arrived.

James Patrick Dunigan, a lean, down-to-earth Texan who went by the name Pat, headed the group of partners from central Texas. Born in 1924, Dunigan was a third-generation oilman and president of Dunigan Tool and Supply Company of Abilene, a tool and supply business for oil and gas operations that provided equipment for pipeline networks and refineries. The other investors came to the partnership with similar backgrounds, but most of the minority owners would play a limited role in the subsequent management of the property.

Dunigan had learned that the Baca Location was on the market in the fall of 1962. He and Joab Harrell, vice president of Dunigan Tool and Supply, arranged a visit to the property during the first days of October. George Savage of the Albuquerque firm Savage and Sganzini, trustees of the Bond Estate, didn't consider the Texas group a good prospective buyer. Savage drove the group to the property, but he assigned the task of leading the tour of the ranch to one of his employees. With little hope that the Texans were serious about the property, Savage stayed at the headquarters area and listened to the World Series on the radio.

Dunigan was drawn to the beauty of the caldera landscape and the opportunities for grazing cattle. He was a wealthy Texas businessman, and in those days every young, successful oilman owned a ranch. At first Harrell was lukewarm on the purchase, but a week after his visit he became enthused about the property. Back in Texas the partners learned of a wildcat well that had been sunk two years before. The drillers were searching for oil, but instead had hit steam. Harrell later said that the geothermal potential of the Baca property was the primary reason for his interest in the purchase. For Dunigan, developing geothermal power was secondary to the property's scenic and grazing value. The Texas group formed the Baca Land and Cattle Company and signed a purchase agreement on December 4, 1962. The deed for the Baca Location No. 1 was transferred on January 1, 1963. The sale price was said to be $2.5 million.[12]

The Texas group immediately made it clear that they had not purchased the property on the speculation that the government wanted it for a park. Surprised and bitterly disappointed, the supporters of Anderson's park proposal weren't sure what to expect from the Texans. To alleviate some of the public's fears, the Baca Land and Cattle Company announced they would delay development until the completion of a suitable master plan for the entire property. Baca Land and Cattle acknowledged that the potential land uses included cattle ranching, recreation, and home sites, and in the end some of the land might be sold to the government.[13]

The sale of the property had taken the wind out of the National Park Service's sails. Undaunted but not optimistic, Clinton Anderson introduced new legislation to authorize the Secretary of the Interior to acquire the Valle Grande tract within the Baca Location. But the window of opportunity had passed and the bill died a quiet death.

Initial reaction in Los Alamos to the Dunigan purchase of the Baca Location was not favorable. With the Texas group talking about development of a possible "Sun Valley-type development," rumors ran rampant. Within two weeks of the announcement of the purchase, the Los Alamos Scientific Laboratory community publication, *The Atom*, sounded the alarm and helped spread rumors about the development of a ski area, home sites, and the "world's largest golf course." The magazine served up a sarcastic cartoon depicting the Jemez Mountains as Little Texas, with the Baca Location transformed into a lakeside resort at the foot of Mount Sam Houston.[14]

James Patrick Dunigan was raised in Texas, served in the Army Air Corps during World War II, then joined his father's business supplying tools and equipment to oil fields. Photo courtesy of the Dunigan family.

Later that spring the *Los Alamos Monitor* reported that Baca Land and Cattle's plans for the property included a ski resort, racetrack, and a resort community. The partners hired architect James Tittle of Abilene and directed him to produce a master plan for the property. As Tittle visited the site by jeep and horseback, his enthusiasm grew. Some local skiers, who for years had eyed the north slopes of Redondo Peak as the location for a new ski resort, loved Tittle's attention to the mountain.

Fueling the fears of unbounded development were photographs of construction on the ranch. Dunigan hired Bob Brown, an Albuquerque general contractor, to build new facilities and by April construction was underway. Just inside the timber near the old Bond Headquarters, crews worked on two A-frame cabins and an eight-bedroom lodge, which Dunigan called the Casa de Baca.

In early May the Albuquerque manager of the Baca Land and Cattle Company, Tully Petty, confirmed that a racetrack in the Valle Grande was indeed possible. Petty went on to reveal plans to drill for steam and build a geothermal power plant on the property. The Los Alamos community feared the worst and grew more suspicious of its new neighbors from Texas.[15]

Dunigan saw that a favorable public opinion was quickly getting away from him. On May 22, 1963, he toured the Baca Location with a reporter and photographer from the *Los Alamos Monitor* and tried to set the record straight.

Dunigan admitted that a racetrack had been considered, but it was only one of many things being discussed. "Anyway, horses can't run at this altitude," Dunigan said.

Nothing else Dunigan said comforted the *Monitor's* readers. The latest plan, Dunigan said, called for the development of shops south of NM Highway 4 that would be leased to concessionaires. Home sites in the same area as the shops, along the southeast edge of the Valle Grande, and on the saddle at the foot of Cerro Grande would be sold and closely regulated.

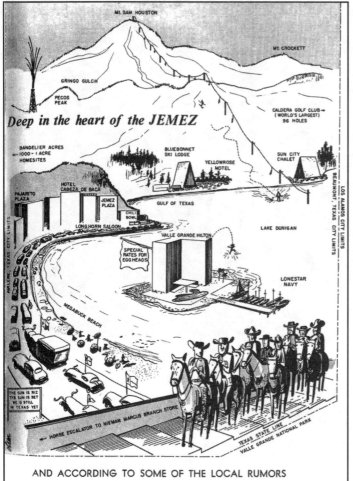

Deep in the heart of the JEMEZ

AND ACCORDING TO SOME OF THE LOCAL RUMORS

"If anyone thinks they are going to come up here and build $2,000 summer cabins, they might as well forget it," Dunigan said.

In the eyes of many, Dunigan's interview brought even worse news. The partners discussed the possibility of a golf course that would be placed north of Highway 4 and in the southwest corner of the Valle Grande. And they had contracted a Denver firm to draft a proposal for a ski area.

Dunigan stressed that all the planning was tentative. He concluded the interview with a consolatory statement. "We may all turn to ranching and run this thing for the next three generations."[16]

In late June 1963 Dunigan again talked to a reporter from the *Los Alamos Monitor*, telling the newspaper that plans to develop recreational facilities on the ranch had been abandoned. A week before, the partners in the Baca Land and Cattle Company met and reached the decision to scrap all development plans and keep the Baca Location simply as a working cattle ranch. Dunigan cited the high cost of construction, labor, and transportation in the central Jemez as the reason for tabling the large-scale development plans. A collective sigh of relief could be felt in Los Alamos.[17]

Dunigan arrived on the Baca Location No. 1 with a commitment to preserve the property as a working ranch while retaining its scenic values. He half-heartedly supported the plans for development as part of the partnership. Within a few months, his point of view prevailed. Dunigan confided in private that he wanted to make the Baca Ranch his life's work. His sincerest desire was to make the Baca an operation that would be a credit to all of northern New Mexico, as befitted the beautiful countryside. In accordance with Dunigan's wishes, by the end of summer the Baca Land and Cattle Company settled down to emphasize the ranching aspect of its name.[18]

The Baca Land and Cattle Company hired cowboys and used the ranch's older buildings as bunkhouses and offices. Cowboy Danny Cupit left his mark on the beam over the front door of the old Otero Headquarters, which was at the time used as a small bunkhouse.

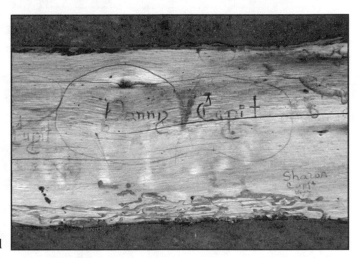

However, the proposed Valle Grande-Bandelier National Park gasped one last breath. In early 1964 New Mexico Senators Edwin L. Mechem and Clinton Anderson reintroduced legislation in Congress that called for the purchase of the Valle Grande for the new park. Pat Dunigan and his partners objected to the proposal and restated that the land was not for sale. The bill authorized $950,000 to purchase the Valle Grande, but Dunigan said that he and his partners had already turned down an offer for $6.5 million on the entire property. Furthermore, in the first year they had made more than $300,000 worth of improvements to their property, almost all of which were within the boundaries of the proposed park. As a result of Dunigan's lack of interest, the park proposal never made it out of committee.[19]

In late 1964 the Baca Land and Cattle Company grazed cattle in the quiet, grassy bowls of the Valles Caldera. But on the surrounding hillsides, chainsaws buzzed and logging trucks thundered through the forests. The sincerity of Pat Dunigan's stewardship of the land was about to be put to the test.

CHAPTER EIGHT
1964 TO 1972

HIGH GRADE TO LOW GRADE: LOGGING THE CALDERA

In 1915 the Redondo Development Company was in financial trouble. In its first six years of ownership, the company's income from the Baca Location amounted to little more than grazing fees on the lease to Frederico Otero. Because of the property's remote location, land sales and logging were not economically feasible. The situation forced the company to take out a mortgage on the property, and payment was due in 1925.

The mortgage holder, Warren Savings Bank of Pennsylvania, was granted certain rights, but the agreement carefully spelled out that the forests of the Baca Location remained in control of Redondo Development. The legal document specified that, "The Redondo Development Company shall have full power to sell, and convey, according to its discretion, the timber growing upon the lands hereby mortgaged...." The company still believed the only way to realize a profit on the Baca Location was through its timber resources.[1]

Small timber firms started commercial logging in the Jemez in late 1800s. Sawmills were scattered throughout the mountain meadows and included small-capacity mills at Vallecitos de los Indios, at Battleship Rock, and in the town of Ponderosa. That name was acknowledgment of the primary resource of the loggers, the orange-barked ponderosa pine. Several logging companies talked of building a railroad into the Jemez Mountains by way of the Cañon de San Diego. The Redondo Development Company hoped to join the logging boom by cashing in on the old-growth stands of ponderosa pines that ringed the valleys of the Valles Caldera. The lack of an efficient way to transport logs out of the mountains was the biggest obstacle, but the company believed that problem would be resolved when the proposed railroad reached Jemez Springs.

The railroad never arrived. Taking a mortgage on the property permitted Redondo Development to hold onto the Baca Location No. 1 until it could sell the timber. An even better solution presented itself when Frank Bond expressed interest in purchasing the property in 1918. Because Bond was focused on grazing in *Los Valles*, the company could sell the land and at the same time carefully retain its interests in the timber. In March of that year, Bond proposed that he purchase the land and give Redondo Development a 50-year option on the timber. Redondo's Edward Wetmore wanted a longer option period, forcing Bond to withdraw his offer. By winter Bond was ready to accept Wetmore's terms. The Redondo Development Company drew up a sales contract for Bond. The company sold the Baca Location No. 1 to Frank and George Bond, but Redondo Development retained a 99-year lease to the timber rights of the property.

Redondo Development clearly believed that someday it could sell the timber on the property. The sale agreement was signed on December 14, 1918, and established Redondo Development's rights to the timber on the Baca Location No. 1 until 2017. The timber rights included ownership of "all the timber trees and wood and increment thereof, standing, growing, lying" on the property. It also guaranteed Redondo Development's right to enter the property at any time, to build roads, telephone lines, mills, and anything else necessary for removing the timber. The deed further stipulated that Bond exercise due care to protect all timber from physical damage and fire and to provide at least three men to ride the range all summer to insure that these conditions were met. Although Bond's interest was primarily in grazing, he would have preferred to own the timber as well as the land.[2]

Over the next six years, Bond ran his sheep operations on the ranch and paid for the property in five installments. The deed to Baca Location No. 1 finally passed into Bond's hand on April 8, 1926. The timber rights, however, still belonged to the Pennsylvania company.

The Redondo Development Company waited another nine years for the opportunity to make a profit on the timber rights. In 1935 the Civilian Conservation Corps constructed the first graded road from Los Alamos to Cuba, making travel through the Jemez Mountains easier than ever before. Around the same time, logging firms developed trucks that were more practical than railroad spurs to haul logs and lumber from the woods. The combination of factors finally made commercial logging of the Baca Location economically viable.[3]

In July 1935, a few weeks before the new road opened, Redondo Development called Franklin Bond at his home in Albuquerque. At the time Bond was in California visiting his father, and Franklin's wife Ethel took the call. With no hint of what was in the works, Ethel suggested that the Redondo representative contact Franklin in California. He never made the call. Within hours, Redondo Development sold their timber rights to the Firesteel Lumber Company. Ethel Bond later said that if she knew what the call was about—and despite the fact that she never interfered with her husband's business—she would have instantly agreed to purchase the timber.[4]

From the start of timber operations on the Baca Locations No. 1, trucks were used to haul large ponderosa pine logs. Photo from the Los Alamos Historical Society Archives.

Robert Anderson Jr. of Firesteel Lumber paid $150,000 for the rights to log the property. As was the company's usual style, Redondo Development's deed for the timber included a maze of legal restrictions. The deed required Anderson to make a down payment, and then demanded strict adherence to the specified payment schedule. Further, the Redondo Development Company was permitted to inspect Firesteel Lumber's books at any time. Otherwise, with its sale of the timber rights the Redondo Development Company

bowed out of the scene and no longer played a role on the Baca Location.[5]

Robert Anderson immediately transferred the timber rights to Abram I. Kaplan, the largest investor in New Mexico Lumber and Timber. This company was currently engaged in logging the Cañon de San Diego Grant to the south. With equipment already in the area, the company quickly began the first extensive logging operations on the Baca Location. The project focused on the pines on Redondo Border and the Banco Bonito lava flow. Before the year was out, most of the entire southwest corner of the property was part of the logging operation. A sawmill in Redondo Meadow handled the logs, and the lumber was shipped on the good downhill grades through Jemez Springs to the railroad landing at Cañones. Anderson reported that 42 million board feet of timber was cut in 1935.[6]

To facilitate its operation, New Mexico Lumber and Timber established a logging camp at the north end of the huge meadow along Redondo Creek immediately south of the peak with the same name. Timber employees came from Texas, Oklahoma, and Arkansas, and the company hired Mexican nationals and a few local residents. The camp was home to 25 employees, some of whom brought their families to live with them. The company built tiny frame houses, placing the structures on skids so they could be moved from place to place according to demand. Other workers lived in log cabins strung out along the creek. The cabins were cramped, measuring only 12 feet by 16 feet. The camp included a mess hall, school, and, until trucks and tractors replaced horses at the job sites, stables. The logging crews worked seven days a week from May to March. Days off came only when the weather kept them from work. There wasn't much to amuse the men at camp, so when they could, they headed down the Cañon de San Diego to Jemez Springs and Billy Mann's bar.[7]

Old-growth pondero-sa pine stands, with an open, park-like appearance, ringed the valleys of the Valles Caldera. It was in these stands that the first logging operations took place.

Magnificent ponderosa pines—with vanilla-scented orange bark, 200 feet tall and over 400 years old—found prime growing conditions at the bases of the volcanic domes in the Valles Caldera. The ponderosas flourished on the gentle slopes that lie above the compacted soils of long-ago drained lakes in the valley floors and below the steep, rocky mountainsides. Frequent ground fires kept the stands open, creating a park-like setting that contrasted sharply with the extensive grasslands a few yards downslope and with the dense forest above.

The easiest, least expensive logging centered on the ponderosa stands. Limitations of equipment and the difficulty of moving logs on steep terrain kept the sawyers off steep slopes. The company constructed rough roads through the grasslands that reached the quality pine stands without requiring extensive engineering plans. Sawyers made their cuts with two-man saws that were most easily used at chest height. Pushing and pulling and using wedges to keep the saw from binding, a team could fell even the largest pines in several hours. (The tall stumps left by the sawyers are distinctive of this era.) Felled trees were skidded—dragged—by teams of horses or by machinery to loading areas. Lacking cranes to lift the logs onto the backs of trucks, the loading areas were often flat landings excavated into hillsides. Even the largest diameter logs could be rolled from the hill onto the flatbed trucks, which sat in the depressions.

By taking the largest, oldest pines, New Mexico Lumber and Timber high-graded the timber resources of the Baca Location. At first it did so with an eye on the future. Not all the trees were harvested, and on all stands a few old giants were left to provide a seed source for regeneration.[8]

In 1940 a financial reorganization turned New Mexico Lumber and Timber into the New Mexico Timber Company. Thomas Patrick Gallagher and his partner A. I. Kaplan of the new company held the timber lease on the Baca Location No. 1. Gallagher came to New Mexico in 1929 and had been success- fully running logging operations for New Mexico Lumber and Timber since his arrival, not only as the company president but also as a heavy investor. The new lessee closed Redondo Camp and moved logging operations to the northwest portion of the Baca Location. New Mexico Timber built more roads and operated several small sawmills in the meadows of this remote corner of the property. Logging on the property continued into and after the war years at El Cajete, the Jaramillo Creek drainage, and along the northern border of the ranch.[9]

From 1935 to 1963 the timber companies logged more than 25,000 acres of the Baca Location. Most of the harvest was ponderosa pine, but about 10,000 acres of spruce-fir and mixed conifer stands were also stripped of the largest trees. The base of the eastern and northern caldera rims, the lowermost slopes of Cerro del Medio, Cerros del Abrigo, and the Cerros de Trasquilar were extensively logged during the later years of this period.[10]

As Pat Dunigan and his partners negotiated for the purchase of the property, logging practices on the Baca Location No. 1 made a dramatic shift. However, the change in cutting operations had nothing to do with the change in ownership.

When the National Park Service pushed its plans for the Jemez Crater National Monument in December 1962, Thomas Gallagher, Jr., of the New Mexico Timber Company reminded the government and citizens who were eagerly awaiting the new national park that his company held the timber rights to the entire Baca property. Gallagher announced that if the government purchased the property, his company would continue its timber operations. Furthermore, the timber man felt that recreational

Old stumps from trees cut down from 1935 through the 1950s are common along the forest boundary with the grasslands. Higher stumps were cut with two-man saws that were more efficient when used at chest height.

use of the land would be incompatible with logging. The only way out of the dilemma would be for the government to buy the timber lease, but Gallagher thought that the government would be unwilling to pay the true value of the lease and that a deal would never be reached.

In response to pointed questions from the *LASL Community News* out of Los Alamos, Gallagher boldly stated that market prices would determine how much future logging would be done on the property. He estimated that most of the timber suitable for lumber—about $5 million worth—would be cut before 1972. Furthermore, Gallagher felt that since he was taking only the largest trees, the scenic beauty of the Valles Caldera was not threatened. At the time, New Mexico Timber was harvesting all pines over 12 inches in diameter, leaving four seed trees per acre.[11]

Several logging camps and cabins were built on the Baca Location No. 1 during the 1930s and 1940s. This cabin ruin near El Cajete is isolated from others of the same time period.

Two events led to a radical shift in New Mexico Timber's outlook. During the first 30 years of logging on the Baca Location No. 1, only large diameter trees suitable for making lumber had been cut. Smaller trees were left standing, not only because they were not suitable for lumber but because state timber laws prohibited cutting trees under a specified diameter. In 1962 the New Mexico legislature redefined what size trees could be legally harvested in the state, reducing the minimum diameter of eligible trees to between five to sixteen inches, depending on the species. New Mexico Timber could now legally cut the smaller sized spruce and fir that grew on the steep slopes of the property. At the time, the company had no market for small logs. Then in early 1963 a new pulpwood mill opened in Snowflake, Arizona. Unlike lumber, pulpwood could come from any diameter tree and was just as easily made from spruce, fir, or aspen as from pine. The Arizona mill made it economically feasible for New Mexico Timber to harvest small trees from the Baca Location No. 1. The legal shift in defining eligible tree size and species meant that all the remaining forests of the Baca Location were of economic value.

Shortly after Pat Dunigan and his partners purchased the Baca Location, Gallagher announced that New Mexico Timber had entered a contract with the Arizona mill to cut millions of dollars worth of pulpwood from his timber lease on the Baca Ranch. Logging on the property was about to move upslope to the spruce-fir and mixed conifer forests on the wooded mountainsides of the Valles Caldera.[12]

To efficiently harvest smaller diameter trees, New Mexico Timber radically changed its logging techniques. Because timber of any diameter could be used for pulpwood, the company abandoned selective harvest and began clearing large areas of timber. The company used cable-logging methods. It built and graded parallel roads every 250 to 300 feet up the hillsides. Cables were tossed from the roads and dragged along the slopes, effectively

Between 1963 and 1971 New Mexico Timber bladed more than 1,000 miles of roads on the Baca Ranch. Map from Craig Allen, USGS Jemez Mountain Field Station.

knocking down all the timber. Once the trees were stripped from the soil, swampers lopped off the branches. Heavy equipment piled the trunks. A convoy of trucks carried off the valuable logs.

Left behind were three- to six-feet high piles of jumbled limbs, brush, and debris. The piles were formidable barriers to livestock and wildlife. The slash piles and remaining snags increased the fire danger in the area to unacceptable levels. Indeed, several fires started on the logged hills in the late 1960s. Noted conservationist Elliott Barker toured the timbered area and said, "It looked like a giant tornado has passed through the area. It is one of the biggest messes I have ever seen." The New Mexico Timber Company appeared eager to make its profit and exit the area as soon as possible.

Early in 1964 Pat Dunigan cried foul to New Mexico Timber. The rancher was sickened as he watched the destructive logging practices on the hills surrounding *Los Valles*. He publicly demanded the logging company reevaluate its techniques and halt the wholesale clearing of stands.

Two relationships influenced Dunigan's perspective not only on logging but also on range management. First was his father-in-law, Clarence Burch.

New Mexico Timber's cable logging practices, spiderweb roads, and slash piles brought Pat Dunigan to file suit in an attempt to halt logging on the Baca Ranch. Photo by Robert Baxter.

Burch was born in Bromide, Oklahoma, in 1906. He grew up on farms and ranches, and developed a love of land coupled with an intense curiosity about man's relationships to the landscape. Educated at Oklahoma A&M (now State), Burch worked as a county extension agent, served as director of the Oklahoma State Water Resources, and ran a small ranch in Mill Creek. Burch's interest in cattle led him to be elected the first president of the Beef Improvement Federation. Always searching for better ways to manage rangelands, Burch pioneered conservation of range resources among ranchers and promoted careful study of the effects of grazing on the land. Burch's efforts were among the first in sustainable rangeland management practices.

Early in his ownership of the Baca Ranch, Dunigan sought Burch's advice. Burch toured the ranch with his son-in-law, observing that over the years the meadows and forests had been hit hard. Burch was emphatic about the logging on the ranch. Dunigan had to find a way to stop the destructive timber methods being used by New Mexico Timber.[13]

Dunigan also spend many days with a former classmate from Fort Worth, Bill Huey. Huey was an experienced resource manager and served for years as the head of New Mexico Department of Game and Fish. Huey advised Dunigan on wildlife management and was instrumental in guiding Dunigan to reduce the number of cattle grazed on the property.

Despite the sage counsel from those around him, without owning the timber rights there was little Dunigan could do short of a lawsuit to stop the destructive practices. On May 12, 1964, the Baca Land and Cattle Company sued the New Mexico Timber Company for damages stemming from its logging practices. Dunigan's lawyers argued that the company failed to take adequate care of the land while it was exercising the terms of its lease. They sought an injunction against further logging and damages for the destruction that had already taken place.

Parallel logging roads on the flanks of Cerro del Abrigo. Photo by Robert Baxter, circa 1970.

Because of the complexities of the issues, the court battle was a long, drawn-out affair. Nevertheless, as the lawyers developed their cases, the timber company continued its daily harvests on the ranch. The logging began on the north side of the caldera's central hills and thus out of sight of the public, but by 1968 had curled around the mounds and was visible from the highway.

Judge Vearle Payne at the Federal District Court in Albuquerque heard Dunigan's two-part suit and issued a ruling in August 1969. Concerning the suit's accusation of inadequate care of the land, Payne found in favor of Dunigan and awarded the rancher $200,000 in damages. Payne cited careless practices on roads and slopes that eroded soil and devalued the landscape. Much to Dunigan's dismay, this payment only covered damages inflicted since the onset of the court actions, and which therefore applied only to about 5,000 acres of the almost 10,000 acres logged in the previous five years. In further support of Dunigan's position, the court also set standards for future logging operations on the ranch that included the installation of water diversion structures on roads and the cleanup of slash piles. The New Mexico Timber Company immediately appealed these rulings that favored Dunigan's position.

1977 aerial photographs clearly show the logging roads cut in the previous decade. Cerro del Abrigo, shown here, was at the center of the logging operations. Photo by the United States Geological Survey.

The second part of Dunigan's suit was more complex and somewhat tenuous. The rancher held that the timber rights granted in 1918 allowed the New Mexico Timber Company to harvest only those trees that were marketable at the time the lease was signed. Such an interpretation would prohibit the timber company from cutting trees under about 50 years old—thus eliminating the harvest of small diameter trees. The judge did not agree with this argument and ruled that New Mexico Timber owned "all of the forest, without limitation, from December 14, 1918." Dunigan appealed this portion of the decision.

The uncertain court situation threw the New Mexico Timber Company into a frenzy. Sensing it might be running out of time, the company cut trees at the appalling rate of 24 million board feet per year. It ceased logging operations elsewhere in the state and threw all its resources into the Baca Location, employing 175 men and operating two mills.[14]

The *Los Alamos Monitor* sent a reporter and photographer to the Baca Location to investigate the status of logging on the property. In November 1970 the paper printed a photograph that stretched across the entire front page. It showed the north face of Cerro del Medio, trees gone, logs scattered about the landscape as if toppled by an explosion, and roads looped across the slopes like contour lines on a map. The front-page story fed the outrage of many observers in Los Alamos. Sam Bailey, New Mexico Timber's forester, defended the company's practices and tried to downplay the devastated appearance of the landscape. The slash, he said, would soon be covered up by second growth forest. Bailey claimed that the extensive roads caused less damage to the hills than other logging techniques. The arguments seemed to convince few readers.[15]

Between 1963 and 1971 New Mexico Timber graded over 1,000 miles of road. Their first cable-logging operations were on the north sides of the ring fracture domes of both caldera-forming eruptions. The hills surrounding the Valle Toledo were hit hardest: Cerros del Abrigo, Cerros de los Posos, Cerro Toledo, and Cerro del Medio were covered with a spaghetti-network of interlocking roads. By 1971 logging occurred on the north side of Redondo Peak and a logging camp was established at the headwaters of Redondo Creek.

In September 1970 the Fifth Circuit Court in Denver heard the appeals from Baca Land and Cattle and New Mexico Timber. The cases required a legion of lawyers and expert witnesses, and the court, finding itself in a difficult situation, took until March 1971 to issue its ruling. In both cases the Court of Appeals upheld the decision of the lower court. In June New Mexico Timber paid $202,278 to Baca Land and Cattle, the amount of the original settlement plus interest.[16]

Dunigan was not satisfied with the court's decision. The rancher directed his attorneys to file suits seeking damages not just on the 5,000 acres dealt with in the original suit, but for the entire 40,000 acres that had been logged by New Mexico Timber. But after seven years of fighting, neither side was particularly excited about continuing the battle for the Baca timber in court. The two sides initiated direct negotiations that led to an agreement signed two days before they were scheduled to return to court. On July 1, 1972, all logging operations by the New Mexico Timber Company on the Baca Location ceased. Dunigan purchased the timber lease from Thomas Gallagher for $1.25 million. A joint press release said, "The transaction settles all litigation between the parties."[17]

Ten years after purchasing the land, Pat Dunigan made yet another considerable investment to protect the remaining forests on the Baca Location. In order to mitigate additional damage from the halted timber operations, Dunigan directed his employees to install erosion control measures on the ranch within and below the timbered areas.

"Bailey defended his firm's logging practices, noting that by far the most common technique used with spruce and fir was clear cutting. He also defended the log gathering method used, saying that 'cable' caused much less damge to young trees than 'cat' logging. 'Cable' logging, however, requires more roads, in fact many more roads."

Los Alamos Monitor *Interview with Sam Bailey of New Mexico Timber, November 1970.*

Over the eight-year battle over the timber operations on the ranch, Pat Dunigan had proved himself a capable and responsible steward of the landscape, both willing and able to back up his words with money and action.

CHAPTER NINE
1973 TO 2000

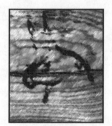

STEAM, COWS, ELK, AND HOLLYWOOD

With the timber issues settled to his satisfaction, Pat Dunigan focused his attention on other facets of his ranchoperations. The Texan and his partners took a broad-based look at the economics of the Baca Land and Cattle Company. Limited, well-managed logging and cattle ranching remained the mainstays of the ranch, but to diversify the ranch Dunigan also sold parcels of lands, operated hunting camps, and permitted Hollywood to use the ranch as a backdrop for films. But Dunigan wasted little time in exploring the possibilities of power generation from steam on the Baca Location No. 1.

The intense heat from the magma chamber lying beneath the Valles Caldera radiates upward from the molten rock toward the surface. The heat dramatically increases the temperature of groundwater flowing deep within the rocks. Some of the heated water finds its way to the surface to form hot springs, but the majority of the groundwater remains superheated deep within the caldera. Tapping into such a reservoir of steam could lead to an inexpensive way to generate electricity.

Confirmation that high-pressure steam existed under the surface of the Valles Caldera happened by accident. In 1960 the Westates Petroleum Company received permission from the Bond family to sink a test oil well near the bubbling seeps in Alamo Canyon, a headwater of Sulphur Creek. The area lies at the top of a structural dome, which is a common location for petroleum reservoirs. As the company drilled through successive layers of rock, instead of an oil gusher they witnessed a jet of superheated water issuing from their drill hole. Disappointed, Westates quickly packed its bags, but its discovery was not forgotten.[1]

The hot fluid that flowed from the Westates well played an important role in the decision of Pat Dunigan and Joe Harrell to purchase the Baca Location No. 1. Arriving in the area with backgrounds in energy production, the Texans were intrigued by the possibilities of commercial geothermal production from the remaining heat of the Valles Caldera. Immediately following their original tour of the property, Dunigan and Harrell headed west to the geothermal developments north of San Francisco where they acquired enough of a background in natural steam energy production to evaluate seriously the potential for drilling on the ranch.

Dunigan could hardly wait to investigate the geothermal potential of the Baca Location No. 1. As soon as the snowpack thinned in the spring of 1963, Dunigan brought a drill rig into the Sulphur Creek area to punch an exploratory hole. Using seat-of-the-pants drilling techniques borrowed from the oil industry, Dunigan quickly struck a source of steam at the first hole, the Baca No. 1 well. The well was capable of generating about 85,000 pounds of steam per hour, but it showed very little water production. Continuing the reconnaissance, the Baca No. 2 well was placed near the junction of Sulphur Creek and Alamo Canyon, and it produced about 60,000 pounds of hot water per hour. Despite a low output from the Baca No. 3 well the next year, Dunigan was encouraged.

"We originally bought the land for its scenic and cattle producing value, but we were not unaware of its geothermal possibilities."

Pat Dunigan in a 1979 interview with the Abilene Reporter News.

Between 1964 and 1970, Dunigan visited geothermal operations in Italy, Iceland, and New Zealand. From his evaluation of the world's best-developed geothermal fields, the erstwhile oilman calculated that delineating the extent of the Baca geothermal resource would require many more wells and outstrip the abilities of his simple operation. Dunigan and Harrell looked for help and found it in Union Oil of California. In the area north of San Francisco known as "The Geysers," Union Oil had developed a system to produce 400,000 kilowatts of power that fed into the California power grid system. Such production from steam wells impressed the Baca owners.[2]

For the next series of wildcat holes, Harrell brought in Dick Dondanville, a geothermal expert from Union Oil of California. Baca Land and Cattle hired the Arapaho Drilling Company from

Farmington, New Mexico, to drill the Baca No. 4 well along Redondo Creek above the idyllic Redondo Meadow. On October 10, 1970,
after a month of drilling without success, the team hit commercial-quality steam. At 5,000 feet below the surface, the well struck
large quantities of 545-degree-Fahrenheit water. Harrell called the
discovery "a big event." Dunigan had high hopes that the project
would supply power to more than a million people in New Mexico.
With the increasing importance of energy exploration on the
ranch, in 1971 ownership of the geothermal resources of the
property was split in half between Dunigan Enterprises and the
Baca Land and Cattle Company.[3]

Carl Ott, head of the Union Oil of California's geothermal
division, liked what he saw in the Baca No. 4 well. On April 19,
1971, the Union Oil Company of California entered an agreement
with the Baca Land and Cattle Company that permitted the
company to explore for steam and develop geothermal energy on
the Baca Location No. 1. The company's decision to take the 99-
year lease on the geothermal resources of the property was based
primarily on the discovery of commercial-quality steam in the
Baca No. 4 well. While he admitted uncertainty, Ott said, "Our
feeling is that it (the steam field) will be quite large," perhaps
enough to produce several million kilowatts of power.[4]

The terms of the lease gave Union Oil the exclusive right to
drill, extract, and sell hot water or steam from the entire property.
Baca Land and Cattle permitted the oil company to use or construct roads, ponds, pipelines, or transmission lines. Union Oil
built a guardhouse and controlled access to the Redondo Creek
drainage.

Encouraged by the early results of the drilling project, the
Public Service Company of New Mexico (PNM) joined Union Oil in
1973. The partners explored ways to turn the steam into commer-
cially available electric power. Over the next five years, they
invested considerable money and resources into developing
inexpensive power. Five years and ten wells later, the total capacity of the combined wells was 320,000 pounds of steam per hour,
enough volume to encourage Union Oil and PNM to seek funding
to pursue construction of a geothermal power plant. Union
Geothermal, a new subsidiary of Union Oil, would provide the
necessary steam and PNM would build a plant and buy the steam
to generate electric power. It was expected that the scheme would
justify the almost $20 million invested in the drilling to date.[5]

The timing of the proposed power plant was perfect. During
the mid-1970s, the United States placed an increasing emphasis on
non-petroleum based energy production. Instability in the Middle
East created a rise in energy prices that led to initiatives to
develop alternative sources of power and decrease dependence
on foreign petroleum. The newly created Department of Energy
(DOE) was overseer of the new projects.

Seeking government support for research and development, Union Geothermal and PNM approached the DOE with their plan for geothermal power generation on the Baca Location No. 1. On July 6, 1978, the partners entered a cooperative agreement with the DOE to finance construction of a 50-megawatt power plant in Redondo Canyon. The parties estimated that they would need to locate another 600,000 pounds of steam per hour to generate electricity at the capacity of the power plant. They hoped to have the power flowing by mid-1982. Because the volume of steam drawn from the wells was finite, the power plant had a projected life of 30 years.[6]

With the support of DOE funding, Union Geothermal and PNM initiated an extensive drilling program to locate more steam and to determine the extent of the reservoir of hot water beneath the surface. Between July 14, 1978, and April 1981, geothermal researchers drilled an additional twelve wells in the Redondo Creek area. It was an ambitious and expensive project. By 1980 the DOE had invested $50 million of public funds into the project and Union Geothermal contributed another $10 million.[7]

Because the project used federal funding, the National Environmental Policy Act required the DOE to prepare an Environmental Impact Statement (EIS). The draft EIS was released in early 1979, and many area residents concerned with natural and cultural resources in the Jemez found the document sorely lacking. The study did not address impacts on Pueblo religion, the effects of large wells on water supplies in downstream communities, or the potential impacts on recreation in the Jemez Mountains.

Responding to the public outcry, the DOE prepared a second, much more substantial EIS that was released a year later. The second study detailed impacts of the power plant and the attending transmission lines on natural features, environmental quality, and cultural resources in the Redondo Creek area and beyond. Addressing many concerns, the study concluded that the impacts on the landscape would be considerable. Between 10 and 20 percent of the canyon of Redondo Creek would be disturbed by construction. Archeological sites would be disturbed, and surrounding recreational activities would suffer. Geothermal development would be incompatible with the National Natural Landmark status bestowed in 1975 on the entire Baca Location No. 1. Overhead transmission lines would cross the Santa Fe National Forest and Bandelier National Monument, adversely affecting the viewscapes of the region.[8]

A month after the report was released, DOE project manager Arthur Wilbur reported that federal approval of the plan had been delayed by the department's lack of experience in documenting potential impacts on the nearby pueblos. Wilbur reported that "a new wrinkle," the Native American Religious Freedom Act, was the largest obstacle. The recently enacted law specified that planning for federal projects must include the potential impacts on Native American religious practices. The environmental impact statement had already reported that the project would interfere with Pueblo religious practices by destroying sacred sites and objects, contaminating or reducing the availability of water for religious practices, and invading the privacy of those using the sites. Given these potential conflicts, the DOE had to decide if national interests would be served by the project. If so, then the project could proceed.

Wilbur believed that the DOE would approve the project despite the finding of infringement on Pueblo religion. "Congress requested this project," Wilbur said. "The country needs it."[9]

At a public workshop in Los Alamos focusing on the issues raised by the power plant, the three partners ran squarely into the conflict with Pueblo religious practices. Although Union Oil representative Joel Robinson felt that Jemez Pueblo's main objection to the project was that "a plume of steam will be visible on Redondo Peak," in fact Pueblo opposition was far more substantial. On a practical level, the Native Americans saw development along Redondo Creek as a threat to the water resources of the downstream pueblos. Pueblo representatives said the project would contaminate the water supply and reduce the flow of the creek and thus the volume of the Jemez River downstream. But the deeper sticking point was spiritual. Jose Lucero of Santa Clara Pueblo summed up the feelings of his people, saying, "The project threatens religion because the entire Valles Caldera is the church of the Indian people." Geothermal energy development on the Baca Location would threaten native religion, destroy their shrines and places of spiritual power, and invade their privacy. Santa Clara Governor Paul Tafoya said the Pueblo would try to stop the project in the legislative arena, and would fight it in the courts if necessary.[10]

Another conflict arose around geothermal development, that of water rights. Union Geothermal let it be known it was seeking additional water rights from landowners around the caldera. Immediately, Pueblo people, ecologists, and residents of the

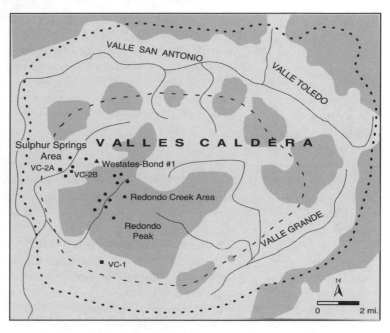

Locations of steam wells on the Baca Location No. 1. Drilling for steam was limited to the western third of the Baca Ranch. The wells were all located in the Sulphur and Redondo Creek drainages.

Jemez River canyon protested, fearing depletion of the flow in the river and in the discharge of the hot springs within Cañon de San Diego. Arguments for both sides were brought before the State Engineer's Office, which ruled in Union Geothermal's favor. The threat of a lawsuit followed.[11]

PNM's last legal hurdle before construction of the power plant was an application for an operating permit. In 1980 PNM made a formal request to the New Mexico Public Service Commission. At the start of the hearing process, the commission refused to hear arguments about religious or environmental issues, claiming that these issues were not within its jurisdiction. After a court ruling declared that the commission indeed had the power to decide those issues, the commission agreed to accept testimony from the partners, the pueblos, energy experts, and environmental groups.

At the expanded hearings, charges and countercharges flew. Arthur Wilbur from the DOE told the commission that any further delay would be damaging not only to the DOE's effort to develop geothermal energy sources but also to the political and economic security of the nation. Ted Davis, president of a group called Save the Jemez, presented a petition with 4,300 signatures opposing the plant. Representatives from the nearby pueblos argued that the power plant would violate sacred sites in the area. PNM countered with the argument that they had found no evidence of religious sites in the area. Jose Lucero explained that after years of persecution, knowledge and practice of the Pueblo religion had become increasingly secret. Redondo Peak was openly acknowledged as an important area, but small shrines were scattered throughout the caldera. The Pueblo people would not reveal where the shrines were located, and Lucero made it clear that the people could not relocate these expressions of their religious roots. The hearings dragged on from September to December, at which time the commission charged each of the parties to the case to prepare final briefs by mid-January 1981. That date was several times pushed later into the year.[12]

The commission never made a decision on the application. On the exploration side of the operation, early optimism had vanished. In May 1981 Union Geothermal announced that its wells could produce only 30,000 pounds of steam per hour, a fraction of what was necessary. The DOE set up a committee to review the project to date. PNM suspended work on the power plant and requested that the public hearing process be halted until it reached a decision on whether or not to resume construction. Additional experiments were conducted through the summer and fall. Still hoping to uncover more steam, Union Geothermal drilled the Baca No. 22 well in December 1981.

But Union Geothermal's partners had seen enough. The cooperative agreement between the Union Geothermal, PNM, and

"It's survival of our people. We cannot lose our identity. We have to have something to leave for our grandchildren and great-grandchildren."

Paul Tafoya, Governor of Santa Clara Pueblo, at a public hearing in Los Alamos, March 1980.

the DOE was terminated on January 22, 1982. In its explanations for abandoning the project, officials downplayed the role of Pueblo rights and environmental concerns. Instead they blamed the inability to obtain at reasonable cost the required volumes of hot water. Richard Engebretsen, a spokesman for Union Geothermal, explained that the lack of permeability of the subsurface rock inhibited the movement of the underground fluids, making it extremely difficult to collect enough water in the wells.[13]

Union Geothermal had 88 years left on its lease of the Baca Location No. 1. Over the next two years, the company drilled two more exploratory wells, but failed to produce an additional large volume of steam. In 1984 Union Geothermal had to take a careful look at its position. One of the terms of the lease agreement called for the company to drill 20,000 feet of well per year or pay the Baca Land and Cattle Company $250,000. Because only limited drilling had occurred early in the year, such a payment would come due at the end of 1984. But the economic climate had changed since 1978 and the price of oil had dropped to its lowest level in a decade. In addition, the downstream pueblos and resort owners filed a lawsuit against Union Geothermal over water rights. In light of the new developments, the company tried to renegotiate a less expensive lease on a smaller portion of the property. Joe Harrell insisted that any exploration lease must cover the entire property. Under these unfavorable conditions, Union Geothermal decided to let go of the lease. Union Geothermal and the Baca Land and Cattle Company signed a letter of agreement on October 4, 1984.[14]

As president of the Baca Land and Cattle Company, Joe Harrell continued to dabble in geothermal exploration. However, the heirs of Pat Dunigan, who still held 87.5 percent of the mineral interest in the property, were not interested in generating new leases.

A different kind of drilling program was started on the Baca Location No. 1 shortly before Union Geothermal pulled out. Flushed with success after the revolutionary discoveries made during its deep sea drilling program, the National Academy of Sciences turned its attention to continental tectonic systems. The academy believed that a detailed study of a hydrothermal system would yield important results and to that end Los Alamos National Laboratory (LANL) geologist Jamie Gardner suggested drilling into the Valles Caldera. With DOE support the National Academy of Sciences approved an ambitious plan to drill at least five holes into the heart of the caldera as part of its Continental Scientific Drilling Program (CSDP).[15]

LANL's Fraser Goff was well qualified to lead the team assigned to drill the first hole. Goff, a specialist in volcanic systems, had spent many years looking at the structure of the Valles

Caldera and its hydrothermal system, including its hot springs. The LANL team selected a site at the vent of the Banco Bonito flow near the southwest corner of the Baca Location No. 1. Recognizing that the CSDP holes would provide them with additional data at no cost, Union Oil gave permission for the LANL

team to sink an exploratory corehole, which was called VC-1. Drilling took place in August 1984 and quickly reached a depth of 2,809 feet. The scientists collected data on the hydrothermal outflow plume of the geothermal area and on the nature of ring fractures. The new information greatly enhanced geologists' understanding of magma systems.[16]

As the time approached for drilling the second CSDP corehole in 1986, Goff found the situation on the Baca Location had changed. Joe Harrell, looking to recoup some of the money lost when Union Geothermal pulled out two years before, wanted LANL to take out a lease on drilling rights for the entire property to the tune of $100,000. Jamie Gardner was given the task of trying to negotiate with Harrell to acquire a more reasonable lease. Even with the support of long-time Dunigan associate Homer Pickens, Gardner was unable to get Harrell to budge from his demands. Frustrated, Gardner and Goff approached John Corbin, the owner of the old

The VC-2A core hole was located at Sulphur Springs. Geologists had to vent steam from the hole to sample fluids from the depths below. Photo by Fraser Goff.

Otero mining claim at Sulphur Springs. Corbin agreed to let the LANL team drill VC-2A on his property.

Sulphur Springs sat just inside the boundary of the Baca Location. To reach the well site the drill rig had to use a half-mile stretch of road on the Baca Location. When the rig reached the gate, Joe Harrell denied the driver access to his road and chased him off. More tedious negotiations followed before Gardner and Harrell reached enough of an understanding to let the drill rig cross the Baca to the corehole site at Sulphur Springs.[17]

As was the case with the previous corehole, the drilling at VC-2A was designed to study both the rocks and the fluids of the subsurface. Extracting core samples was routine, but the scientists had to wake a sleeping dragon to get a look at the fluids. When the well reached a depth of 1,600 feet and temperatures of 210 degrees Celsius, the geologists were in for some excitement as they turned to explosives and high pressures to coax the fluids to vent.

The hydrothermal system was underpressured. The drill hole would fill with fluid, but the team had to load the holes before they would flow toward the surface. A perforation gun—a pipe loaded with a small amount of explosives—was lowered down the casing and detonated. The charges blew holes in the casing and the surrounding rock, and water flowed into the hole. To permit pressure to build inside the hole, the well was capped overnight. When the geologists turned on the valve the next day, the rapid depressurization inside the well caused the top of the accumulated fluids to boil. On the surface, the well turned into a geyser, spewing steam and water to heights up to 100 feet and roaring like a jet engine. The rain that fell from the plume was loaded with silica and destroyed the windows and paint of any vehicles parked too close. After a few minutes, the flow stabilized and the team could divert the eruption into their test equipment.[18]

Goff drilled one more scientific hole in the caldera before the funding dried up. Corehole VC-2B was drilled in 1988, and it was the deepest, hottest, continuously cored well in the world. By the time they were done, the LANL geologists had reached a depth of about 6,000 feet and temperatures of 300 degrees Celsius. [19]

Built by Franklin Bond for Sam and Bertilla Hill in the late 1940s, this small cabin served as a bunkhouse and office for cowboys on the Baca Ranch.

Although the Dunigan family never owned more than a few cattle, cows continued to play an important role on the ranch. Pat Dunigan leased the grazing rights to ranchers from Texas who trucked their herds into the Valle Grande and Valle San Antonio in early May. Ranch hands confined the cattle to corrals for four to five days to permit the cows to adjust to the high altitude and to weed out the sick animals. Before they were released to the grazing pastures, the cows were weighed. After the roundup in September, the cows were again

put on the scales. The grazing fee for each animal was based on its weight gain. Up to 8,000 head grazed on the high meadows for the brief mountain summer.[20]

Early in his ownership Dunigan sought advice from his boyhood friend from Texas, Bill Huey, the head of the New Mexico Department of Game and Fish. The two rode the rangelands on the ranch and decided to adjust the season of grazing to protect the cool-season grasses. By delaying the arrival of cattle until May, these important range species had an opportunity to become better established.[21]

When Pat Dunigan arrived in 1962, he didn't believe that horses could run well at an altitude of 8,400 feet. Years of experience on the ranch led him to an experiment. Dunigan wanted to see if training racehorses at high altitude could improve their ability to run at sea level. In 1977 Dunigan built a large stable for thoroughbreds about a mile north of the headquarters area and on the western border of the Valle Grande. The stable enclosed 18 stalls in two parallel rows. Paddocks enclosing many acres extended from the stable area toward Jaramillo Creek. A one-bedroom apartment was attached to the stable so that trainers never had to be far from their charges. However, Dunigan's death in 1980 ended the experiment with inconclusive results.[22]

As many as 6,000 elk summer on the ranch and use aspen groves in the surrounding mountains as winter range. Photo by John Hogan.

The grasslands and forest of the Baca Ranch brought other opportunities and problems. The modern symbol of the Baca Location No. 1, elk, was not an important part of the fauna of the ranch until the late 1960s. Elk were extinct in New Mexico by 1910. In 1947 the New Mexico Department of Game and Fish released 49 elk from the Yellowstone region in the Rio de las Vacas drainage

west of the Baca Location No. 1. The herd fared well in the grasslands of the Jemez Mountains, but by 1961 the herd had grown only to a population of about 200. Fifty-eight elk from Jackson Hole, Wyoming were brought to the Jemez in 1964 and 1965. The population increased at a slow, steady rate until 1977. In June of that year, the 25,000-acre La Mesa fire burned in the ponderosa pine forests on the Pajarito Plateau at Bandelier National Monument. The fire converted the forest into grassland and opened up considerable winter habitat for the Jemez elk population. With favorable climatic conditions, the elk herd expanded to about 7,000 in 1989. In 2001 it was estimated that between 4,000 and 6,000 elk used the Baca Ranch for summer range.[23]

As the elk herd increased, Pat Dunigan realized that cattle and elk competed for the same basic resource in the *valles*. Seeing elk as an important part of the ecosystem of the ranch, in 1972 Dunigan ordered a decrease in the number of cattle grazed on the property. Dunigan cut the number from about 8,000 to between

4,000 and 6,000. The increase in the availability of food brought herds of elk into the Valle Grande each summer and fall. For those traveling on New Mexico Highway 4 through the ranch, elk watching became a popular activity. During the rutting season, bulls with impossibly heavy, spreading antlers herded their harems of cows in full view of the highway. On fall mornings and evenings, visitors along the road sat quietly to listen to as many as twenty different bulls bugling from various locations around the valley.

Elk hunting greatly increased in popularity during the Dunigan years. The Baca Land and Cattle Company offered guided hunts through a private operator. The Dunigan Casa de Baca served as the hunting lodge for those who were willing to try to bag a trophy bull for a $10,000 fee. A total of 265 elk permits were granted in 1998.

By the mid-1990s, signs of elk overpopulation were plentiful. The moist meadows of the Valle Grande and other valleys showed signs of heavy use. Aspen groves ringing the valleys were scarred with elk tooth marks. Rutted elk trails fanned out from the meadows through the surrounding forests. In some cases, elk traffic had damaged archeological sites. With only a small population of mountain lions remaining as natural predators, indications are that the elk population will continue expanding.[24]

The Dunigan family guest house, originally called Casa de Baca, was used as a lodge during the elk hunts. Designed by James Tittle in 1963, the lodge has eight bedrooms surrounding a central living room with a floor-to-ceiling stone fireplace.

Through the 1960s, the original square shape of the Baca Location remained intact. The inholding at Sulphur Springs and three small homestead claims along the west and southern borders were the only lands within the boundaries that were not part of the Dunigan property. Over the next two decades, additional small parcels of land were nibbled from the property.

Along the Baca Location's eastern border, the Los Alamos Ski Club operates the small Pajarito Mountain Ski Area. In 1971 the club initiated expansion plans and eyed a small tract on the Baca Location that bordered their property and that would allow the construction of a new lift to the top of Pajarito Mountain. The addition would open up a significant area of north-facing slopes to skiing, accommodate the increasing numbers of skiers at the area, and add both more difficult and easier terrain. Because of the uncertainty of the timber status on the Baca Location, Dunigan was reluctant to sell. Once the timber rights were transferred to

Dunigan in 1972, the ski club reopened the discussion. The sale was finalized in February 1975, and 165 acres along the Baca's eastern boundary were sold to the ski club.[25]

Dunigan's largest land sale became the only section of the Baca Location to pass into the hands of the National Park Service. The destructive logging operations run by New Mexico Timber on the Baca Location made Bandelier National Monument's management uneasy. Bandelier officials feared that if logging spilled over into the Upper Frijoles watershed, repercussions would be felt downstream, potentially damaging the canyon-bottom pueblo ruins for which the national monument is famous. Even after the timber rights went to Dunigan, the NPS pursued the acquisition of the upper watershed to exclude it from either logging or grazing.

The NPS proceeded carefully, contacting Dunigan in 1973 to explain its position on the Upper Frijoles Tract. Dunigan understood the concerns of the NPS and was immediately willing to sell the parcel. In 1975 the Department of the Interior offered Dunigan $1,350,000 for 3,076 acres, but several issues delayed the sale. First, questions surrounded the geothermal lease for the entire ranch to Union Oil of California. The company gave a verbal commitment that it would release its claim on the parcel, which was far removed from the sources of heat it was investigating. Joab Harrell held an undivided mineral interest on the entire Baca Location No. 1. In order to simplify the sale of the Upper Frijoles Tract to the satisfaction of the NPS, Dunigan agreed to acquire all the mineral rights to the tract. Harrell agreed to exchange his mineral interest in the Upper Frijoles Tract for a 12-acre tract on the south side of New Mexico Highway 4. Dunigan added one stipulation to the sale: until the area was enclosed by a fence, the horseshoe-shaped parcel would remain closed to the public. Bandelier agreed and the sale was completed on January 28, 1977.[26]

Harrell and his wife built a small house on their 12-acre property and lived there seasonally until 1988. Two other small parcels of land within the boundaries of the Baca Location were sold to private owners in 1986 and 1987.

In 1970 Dunigan opened the ranch to Hollywood director Henry Hathaway for the filming of a classic-style western, *Shoot-out*. The film crew built a small, two-building set on the edge of the Valle Grande near a stand of old-growth forest. Gregory Peck starred in the movie as an honorable bank robber who serves his jail time and then, upon his release, seeks revenge on his former partner. A widow who lives in the simple frame house on the set befriends Peck, and the Valle Grande is an essential feature of several scenes. Because the set was simply a shell, the interior scenes were filmed elsewhere. Later, the Dunigans finished the inside, and the interior was used for two other films.

In the next 30 years the Baca Location No. 1 formed the backdrop for at least eight additional films. None of the films were classics and all were westerns. Opening the ranch to film crews was not a money-making proposition for the Dunigan family. In fact, with the extra ranch hands required to guide, supervise, and entertain the guests, the Dunigans usually lost money on filmmaking on the property. Nevertheless, the family not only had fun playing backdrop for Hollywood, but also provided a valuable service to the New Mexico Film Commission.[27]

The National Broadcasting Company arrived in 1977 to film *Peter Lundy and the Medicine Hat Stallion*, based on a novel by children's writer Marguerite Henry. In the film the Valle Grande played the role of the route of the Pony Express near South Pass in Wyoming. The cowboy cabin on San Antonio Creek, along with its corrals, was converted into a way station for the mail route. A small set, the Box Elder Station, was constructed at the foot of Cerro Piñon, but was destroyed as part of an Indian attack in the film. No one in the film crew seemed to object to the backdrop of Cerro del Abrigo with its freshly cut logging roads.

In 1993 actor and director Terence Hill brought a crew to shoot *Fight Before Christmas* (later known as *Troublemakers*) at the ranch. The filmmakers built a large ranch house on a knoll overlooking the Valle Grande that is easily seen from New Mexico Highway 4. The inside of the set was considerably roughed up during the drawn-out, slapstick fight scene that gave the film its name. For the movie's important Christmas tree, the crew planted a huge ponderosa pine in the middle of the grasslands next to the set. Supported by invisible steel cables, the tree was bedecked with lights for the film's final scene.

The same set was used when Tom Selleck rolled onto the property in 1996 to film a story about an embittered Confederate soldier trying to make a new start in *Last Stand at Saber River*. Converted this time into a general store occupied by the film's villain, the large set is shown in many scenes, but the film took no advantage of the backdrop of the Valle Grande. The crew of the TV mini-series *Buffalo Girls* used the property to better advantage in 1993. The series, which starred Anjelica Huston, Melanie Griffith, Jack Palance, and Sam Elliott, focused on Huston as Calamity Jane. A new movie set was constructed in the Jaramillo Valley at

The set for the movie Fight Before Christmas *sits on a ridge overlooking the Valle Grande near New Mexico Highway 4. Visitors to the area frequently mistake it for one of the original ranch houses on the Baca Location No. 1.*

Movies Filmed on the
Baca Location No. 1,
1971 to 2003

Title	Star	Year	Location
Shootout	Gregory Peck	1971	Headquarters area
Peter Lundy and the Medicine Hat Stallion (TV)	Leif Garrett	1977	Valle Jaramillo, Valle Grande
The Gambler (TV)	Kenny Rogers	1982	Headquarters area
Fight Before Christmas	Terrance Hill	1992	Near entrance road
Buffalo Girls (TV)	Anjelica Huston	1994	Cerro Piñon
Last Stand at Saber River	Tom Selleck	1997	*Fight Before Christmas* set
The Missing	Tommy Lee Jones	2003	Near entrance road

the foot of Cerro Piñon, this one a small ghost town consisting of three false fronts. Several winter scenes featured the forests of the

Valles Caldera. The film concludes with Huston's voice-over saying she is headed back home into her "beloved Rocky Mountains" as she rides into the Valle Grande.

After the Baca Ranch was sold to the federal government and became the Valles Caldera National Preserve in 2000, filming continued on the ranch. In 2003, amid some controversy derived from the fact that the general public was not permitted easy access to the property, film crews under the direction of Ron Howard arrived. Near the set built ten years before for the *Fight Before Christmas*, the crew from Local 490 built a barn to serve as a backdrop for the movie. Described as a chilling suspense thriller, *The Missing* brought well-known actor Tommy Lee Jones and the versatile actress Cate Blanchett to the ranch. The film, set in New Mexico in 1886, follows Blanchett as a young woman who is raising her two daughters in an isolated and lawless wilderness. One of her daughters is

The ghost town movie set constructed for Buffalo Girls *stands in a small valley just off the Valle Grande.*

Window of the set for The Missing, *inscribed by members of Local 490.*

kidnapped by a psychopathic killer with mystical powers and she seeks out her estranged father, played by Jones, to rescue the girl.

The set for the film The Missing *takes full advantage of the backdrop of the Valle Grande. Cerro La Jara is in the near background, and Redondo Peak is on the skyline.*

CHAPTER TEN
1998 TO 2000

THE ROAD TO PRESERVATION

Over time Pat Dunigan became deeply attached to the Baca
Ranch. Under his father-in-law's tutelage, he relished the use of
the property as a working ranch. The rancher also appreciated
the landscape for the unique geological structure that it is. In 1975
Dunigan completed the paperwork to have the Valles Caldera
listed as a National Natural Landmark. Such a listing came with
the expectation—but no legally binding requirements—that
Dunigan would preserve the entirety of the property. The National
Natural Landmark designation recognized the property's "out-
standing illustration of the works of volcanism."[1]

After the timber issue was settled, the National Park Service
(NPS) again had its eyes on the Baca Location. In August 1978
Dunigan invited Deputy Assistant Secretary of the Interior David
Hales and John Cook of the Southwest Region of the Park Service
to tour the ranch. The NPS officials outlined a possible acquisition
strategy and management plan. Dunigan liked what he saw in
terms of the protection of the landscape afforded by the plan, as
well as the possible tax advantages for him. The rancher traveled

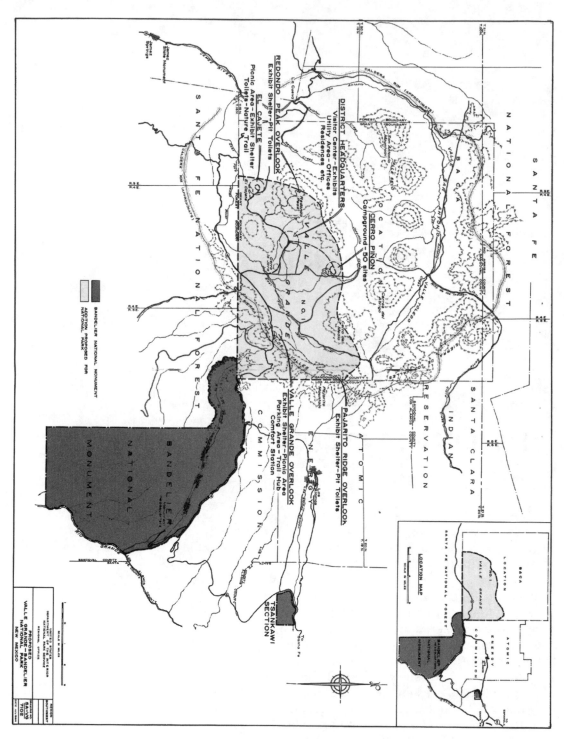

The 1979 planning document for the National Park Service acquisition of the Baca Ranch was a detailed study. The NPS proposed roads, hotels, campgrounds, and a visitor center within the caldera. From the NPS Study of Alternatives.

to Washington to arrange a discussion with NPS Director William Whalen. Whalen had other priorities, however, and passed Dunigan off to one of his assistants. The rancher felt that the NPS was not taking his offer seriously and withdrew his offer to sell.[2]

Congress went ahead with its plan for funding a Valles Caldera National Park. In 1979 the Department of the Interior released a "Study of Alternatives" as part of a special report to Congress designed to again investigate the possibilities of acquiring the ranch. The report cited several ongoing threats to the Baca Location: possible development of seasonal home subdivisions; geothermal exploration which might severely damage the fragile landscape along Redondo Creek; the impact of proliferating elk populations; and logging or grazing at higher levels by future owners, causing further damage to the grasslands and forests.

One of the proposed alternatives was a joint management plan that included the State of New Mexico and the United States Fish and Wildlife Service (USFWS). The USFWS studied the property and outlined a preliminary plan for the management of the elk herds. However, the clout of the USFWS couldn't stand up to that of the old local antagonists, the U. S. Forest Service and the NPS.[3]

The proposed alternative for management by the two agencies drew heavily on the master plan for the aborted Jemez Crater National Monument. The two agencies would divide the land, with 30,745 acres of the Valle Grande going as an addition to Bandelier and the remaining acres merging with the Santa Fe National Forest. The NPS drew plans for the interpretive thrust on the new monument. The proposal called for paving the road that crossed the Valle Grande from State Highway 4 to the headquarters area, where a visitor center would be built. From the visitor center, the jeep track that climbed over a saddle on South Mountain would be developed to take visitors to El Cajete. The NPS also saw an opportunity to interpret geothermal resources along Redondo Creek.

But Dunigan was not talking to the NPS. In 1979 he began negotiations with the USFS. The rancher was looking for a way to develop his estate and leave a trouble-free legacy for his three sons. He liked the idea of USFS ownership because the agency's multiple use mandate would permit the use of any geothermal energy that could be mined. Appraisals of the property were completed and the two parties established conditions for the sale. One stipulation was that the USFS close all the old logging roads that were not needed for fire protection. In Washington the USFS arranged for funding. The Nature Conservancy would purchase the property, then sell it to the USFS. Dunigan set up a trust for his family. However, one of the sticking points of the negotiations was that initially Dunigan wanted to keep a 1,000-acre tract encompassing the headquarters area of the ranch as an estate for his three sons. Government officials balked at this idea and the talks bogged down. In early 1980 Joab Harrell was under the impression that Dunigan had decided not to sell the ranch, but others like Bill Huey believed that the Baca Ranch was about to become public land.[4]

The chance of federal ownership came to a tragic end on February 17, 1980, when Pat Dunigan collapsed and died of a heart attack. The majority ownership of the ranch passed into a trust set up for Dunigan's young sons, and the trustees were not interested in selling the property. A national park in the Jemez Mountain seemed snakebit. Once again, an unfortunate circumstance derailed years of planning.

Save the Jemez proposed an ambitious plan to protect the natural and archeological resources of the Jemez region from Cuba to Los Alamos, and from Jemez Springs to Chama.

After a seven-year hiatus the Baca Location No. 1 again became the focus of a proposal for a new national park. The impetus for this round of discussion was a high-voltage transmission line that was a leftover from the geothermal exploration era. The original plan for the geothermal plant included a 345-kilovolt transmission line to Los Alamos. Even without the geothermal power plant, the Public Service Company of New Mexico (PNM) was interested in the line. PNM was updating its high-voltage lines in northern New Mexico and needed a new route across the Pajarito Plateau and the Jemez Mountains to complete the transmission system. In 1985 PNM proposed two alternatives for the so-called Ojo Line Extension. One route followed an existing route along the Chama and Rio Grande valleys; the other route took a shortcut from Coyote to Los Alamos by twice crossing the rim of Valles Caldera and passing through the Baca Location No. 1.

Opponents of the Ojo Line included the NPS, the USFS, and the New Mexico Department of Game and Fish. The nearby pueblos objected on the grounds of environmental degradation and infringement on religious freedom. The final environmental impact statement completely glossed over the objections of the numerous opponents, who were outraged. The State of New Mexico filed a lawsuit, and others threatened to file

Proposed Plan for the Jemez Mountains

Gallina Culture National Archeological Preserve

Jemez National Recreation Area

Cuba

Jemez Mountains National Park

Los Alamos

Jemez Springs

Jemez National Archeological Preserve

suits as well. Although never formally withdrawn, the Ojo Line
Extension was quietly dropped from discussion.[5]

Ted Davis, president of Save the Jemez, a grassroots activist
group opposed to development of a geothermal power plant,
sought a permanent solution to the continual threats to the Valles
Caldera and surrounding mountains. To protect the mountains for
the future, Save the Jemez proposed the establishment of a
125,000-acre national park with the Baca Location No. 1 as the
centerpiece. In the plan, the Valles Caldera would be combined
with Bandelier National Monument to form the park, and three
"National Archeological Preserves" with a total of about 300,000
acres would be transferred from the Santa Fe National Forest into
the hands of the NPS. In the first draft of the proposal, none of the
land in the park or the preserves would be open to logging or
grazing. Save the Jemez wanted to remove as much land as
possible from management under the multiple-use policy of the
USFS. The proposal, written in the form of a legislative bill, leaked
prematurely before the group had a chance to consult with either
of the two agencies.[6]

One of the proposed archeological preserves completely
surrounded the town of Jemez Springs. Opposition from that
community was immediate and universal. A counter-group, Save
U.S. from Save the Jemez, called a meeting in the local high school
gym that was attended by about 700 opponents to the park plan.
Ted Davis, who had earlier collected more than 4,000 signatures
on a petition opposing a geothermal power plant in the area,
painfully watched as Jemez community members spoke vehemently in support of traditional uses of the land. But the audi-
ence's biggest round of applause was saved for Tom Berry, the
Baca Ranch foreman, who said, "Been a rumor going around that
the Baca's for sale, and it's not for sale."[7]

Northern New Mexico Congressional Representative Bill
Richardson supported the public acquisition of the Baca Location
No. 1 and gathered a small task force to look at the situation. The
task force quickly concluded that until the owners were contacted
directly, there was no justification for pursuing the park proposal.
A week later New Mexico Senator Pete Domenici intervened.
Citing the strong opposition in the local communities, the senator
directly asked Save the Jemez to withdraw the proposal.

"It clearly does not have a chance of becoming law," Senator
Domenici said. "It is well beyond anything that we would seriously
consider."[8]

Two weeks later the Dunigan family killed the last vestige of
hope for Save the Jemez, the NPS, and others. Representative
Richardson met with Andrew Dunigan on March 26 and asked if
the family was interested in selling the Baca Location No. 1.
Dunigan said no, but assured Richardson that the ranch would
continue to be properly managed to protect its unique resources.[9]

"We want it thrown out. We don't want Save the Jemez representing the people who live here and saying how our forests should be managed. The majority of the people who live in these mountains make their living from them."

Lou Steinmasel, editor of the Jemez Valley Voice, *February 1987*

Although the Save the Jemez proposal was soundly drummed out of town, the 90-year dream of public ownership of the Baca Location No. 1 wouldn't die. As part of a land dispute settlement with the Dunigan family, a 1990 federal legislative directive charged the Forest Service with the task of studying the property to support sound decisions regarding the pursuit of public acquisition of the Baca Ranch.

A series of incidents starting more than two decades earlier led to the 1990 directive. In 1966 the USFS had negotiated with Pat Dunigan to acquire a jagged parcel of land along the northern boundary of the Baca Location. The USFS wanted the strip of land to provide access to remote portions of the Santa Fe National Forest, and the two parties worked out a deal. In exchange for 970 acres, the USFS gave Dunigan the La Majada Grant near Cochiti. Located south of La Bajada Mesa, the grasslands of the grant were considered nonessential to the Forest Service mission. The trade was approved without incident, but after Dunigan sold a part of the grant in 1979, a problem arose. In 1982 the purchaser of the parcel discovered that Santo Domingo Pueblo claimed some portions of the La Majada property. The Dunigan family reached a settlement with the purchaser several years later but filed a lawsuit against the USFS seeking damages. Public Law 101-556 resolved the dispute in 1990. That public law also called for a study to report on the Baca Location No. 1's significant attributes, acquisition options, and the probable cost of the purchase. Because the property was not actually for sale, the study part of the law aroused minimal publicity.[10]

The Baca report detailed the characteristics of the property, the real estate issues associated with it, and listed the options for acquisition. Without making a recommendation, the study listed arguments for and against public ownership. Supporting arguments offered the standard goals of protecting the unique landscape and cultural resources, and opening the land for public recreation. The list of arguments against the purchase were several: the property was too expensive, the federal government already owned too much land in the West, and federal management would damage the land more than continued management by the current owners. The study wisely offered the observation that "Public acquisition of the Baca cannot be approached without also discussing how the property might be managed."

Over the years management issues, interagency competition, and funding had always been the key factors in the failure of attempts at acquisition. While the Baca report collected dust on shelves in Washington, D.C., and in Santa Fe, talk of acquiring the Baca Location No. 1 faded away.

In early 1997 Andrew and Michael Dunigan again stirred up Baca talk in Washington, D. C., by visiting a high-ranking official in the USFS for the purpose of beginning preliminary discussions on selling their ranch. Because federal law states that the USFS cannot purchase land in Arizona and New Mexico without Congressional legislation, the USFS directed the brothers to the New Mexico delegation. During the next few weeks, the Dunigans went to the offices of Senators Pete Domenici and Jeff Bingaman. To honor their father's wishes, the Dunigans offered the government the exclusive option until the end of 1998 to buy the land. Domenici was interested but reluctant because he saw little to no chance of success in seeking the large funding required to purchase the property. The prevailing attitude among Western members of Congress was that the federal government already held enough land and they saw no reason that the Baca Ranch should be added to the list of federal land holdings.[11]

In the fall of 1997 the USFS brought the Baca Ranch to the top of its priority land acquisition list. Senator Jeff Bingaman introduced legislation on September 24 to authorize the purchase of the Baca Ranch by the USFS. In announcing the bill, Bingaman echoed the arguments of his predecessor, Clinton Anderson. "The Baca Location No. 1—famous in New Mexico as the Valle Grande— has been rightly compared to Rocky Mountain National Park or the Grand Canyon in terms of its natural splendor and significance to our country," Bingaman said.

Senator Pete Domenici declined to co-sponsor Bingaman's bill. Domenici's reluctance stemmed from the cost to taxpayers, especially when the federal government already owed millions of dollars for unfinished land acquisitions. He also cited the existence of several million acres in New Mexico and the rest of the West that were deemed surplus by federal agencies.[12]

New Mexico Senator Jeff Bingaman pushed long and hard for federal acquisition of the Baca Location No. 1.

Senator Bingaman, however, stayed true to his quest to purchase the land for the American people. To drum up support, the Senator used the property as its own best spokesperson, arranging a tour of the ranch for officials from the Departments of Agriculture and the Interior. On the tour the officials were all impressed by the landscape and praised the Dunigans for restoring the land from past abuses.

"Over the last 35 years, we've sought to manage it in a way that's environmentally sustainable," Andy Dunigan told a reporter from the *Albuquerque Tribune*. "These are values that my brothers and father held to be very important."[13]

Not unexpectedly, however, given the political climate of fiscal conservatism that prevailed in Congress in 1997, the Bingaman bill did not advance far. When the Clinton Administration's attempts to secure complete funding for the ranch purchase failed, President Bill Clinton committed $20 million from the Land and Conservation Fund for a down payment on the property. Leases for gas and oil extraction on the Outer Continental Shelf generate about $1 billion per year to this fund, with dollars to be used exclusively for the purchase of federal lands. Money had been accumulating in the fund since 1980 and in 1996 it held $11 billion.[14]

In the private sector, regional and national environmental groups banded together to form the Valles Caldera Coalition. The group actively supported the public purchase of the Baca Ranch, a factor that was of critical importance for obtaining Land and Conservation Fund money to complete the purchase. Through early 1998 the coalition waged an intense campaign to educate officials in Washington on the significance of the Baca Location to regional ecosystems. The influential group caught the ear of the entire New Mexico delegation, including Senator Pete Domenici.

By mid-1998 the government was feeling pressure to move on the purchase of the Baca Location No. 1. The Dunigans' offer of first option to the government would lapse at the end of the year. The Republican House and Senate Interior Appropriations Committees tied up the $20 million down payment earmarked by the Clinton administration and approved by both houses of Congress until they received an appraisal on the land. Pressure grew as the national media reported on the proposed Baca sale almost weekly. Private developers began contacting the Dunigans about buying the property. If a down payment were not approved by the end of the Congressional session in October, the Dunigans admitted that they would consider selling to another party. Brian Dunigan believed housing developers would be first in line. "In my opinion, that is the highest and best use," Dunigan said. "We're only giving Congress until the end of this session. They can do what they want to. It's just always been our desire for the people of the United States to have this property."[15]

The possibility of public acquisition of the Baca again looked grim. In June House Republicans rejected the proposed budget for land acquisition in the West, a move that directly affected the Baca purchase. To bypass that appropriation problem, Representative Bill Redmond of the New Mexico Third Congressional District joined Senator Pete Domenici in drafting a bill that would require the sale of surplus federal lands in the West and use the income to purchase the Baca Ranch.[16]

Before the Domenici-Redmond bill was complete, Redmond interjected an alternative plan. The conservative Redmond suggested cutting $20 million from the appropriation for the controversial National Endowment for the Arts (NEA) and using the funds for the down payment for the Baca purchase. The move got the attention of Senator Bingaman, who was pleased to see Redmond's support for the purchase. "But I am puzzled by the proposal to raid the NEA when the money for the Baca is already available in the Land and Water Conservation Fund," Bingaman said. Receiving criticism from all directions, Redmond withdrew his proposal before the end of the week.[17]

The proposed acquisition needed the unqualified support of the influential Republican Pete Domenici. New Mexico's senior senator searched for a way to acquire the Baca Location No. 1 while adhering to his staunch principles on fiscal responsibility and winning the support of his fellow members of Congress. More importantly, the senator wanted a solution that would not conflict with his growing distrust of the way public lands were managed. His staff initially investigated making the ranch part of the Jemez National Recreation Area or creating a new unit of the Bureau of Land Management. But a recent solution to a similar dilemma in California was fresh on its mind and led to a different scheme. The core of the staff's proposal had two components: an experimental management system, and the requirement that the property would be maintained in part as a working ranch.[18]

Domenici's staff sketched out a management plan for the Baca Ranch modeled on the unique system at the Presidio Trust. Established in 1996, this executive agency of the federal government partners with the NPS to preserve and enhance the Presidio section of the Golden Gate National Recreation Area in San Francisco. Seeking a way to manage a historic district in a financially stable way, the California delegation and the NPS hit upon the idea of a trust. The seven-member board of directors is charged with preserving the historic structures and character of the Presidio district with a minimum impact on the federal treasury and with a federally mandated goal to become financially self-sufficient by 2013. Domenici and his staff discussed whether this method of management could be applied to a natural area and decided the idea was worth a try.[19]

The support of New Mexico Senator Pete Domenici was crucial to the federal acquisition of the Baca Ranch.

In late July 1998 Senator Domenici flew aboard Air Force One from Washington. D. C. to Albuquerque with President Clinton. In the course of the flight, the two men planned to discuss a pair of issues: nuclear nonproliferation and the acquisition of the Baca Ranch. Domenici joked that nonproliferation would be by far the shorter discussion. Somewhere over the Midwest, the senator proposed the trust management model to the president. Clinton was intrigued and directed his staff to work with the senator on developing the idea. For once the wheels of government turned quickly, and by the end of the next week, the New Mexico congressional delegation and Clinton's staff had a general outline of the trust proposal. Domenici went public with his proposal and, despite some skepticism, the Baca acquisition looked as if it were finally going to succeed. Dave Simon, southwest regional director of the National Parks and Conservation Association, did nothing to hide his enthusiasm. "All I wanted for Christmas was an old volcano, and it does look like we're going to get it," Simon said. After years of work drumming up support for acquisition of the Baca Ranch, Senator Bingaman praised his fellow senator. "I compliment Senator Domenici on this proposal," he said. "I think it's a very good proposal."[20]

A host of details needed to be worked out. New Mexico delegation staffers and the White House laboriously worked through complex negotiations that involved the Justice Department, pueblos, and the president himself, who proved surprisingly knowledgeable about the property. One detail loomed large: funding for the purchase.

Far from a pristine landscape, the Baca Ranch held many signs of past uses. Here, a beaver dam in the Rio de los Indios lies abandoned after the forest upstream was disturbed by logging.

With the sole purpose of getting the language of the proposal before Congress for the first time, at the very end of the 105th Congress the New Mexico delegation introduced a version of the legislation that included the trust proposal. Although the bill never came up for vote in that session, before it adjourned Congress approved the $20 million of Land and Water Conservation funds for a down payment.[21]

But for the supporters of the Baca purchase, the roller coaster ride wasn't even close to being over.

In early 1999 negotiations with the Dunigan family broke down. Because of keen public interest in the acquisition of the Baca Location No. 1, it was difficult to keep some of the family's confidential information out of the public record. When the appraisal of the property was complete, the Dunigans argued that releasing specific information about the value of timber and mineral resources on the property would jeopardize their interests if the sale to the government fell through. But open government laws required that some of the data be made public. The

USFS assured the family that the existing legal protections had never compromised a seller's position. Not satisfied that their concerns would be addressed, on January 7, 1999, the Dunigans abruptly withdrew their offer to sell the ranch to the government.

The hopes of the supporters of the acquisition faded quickly, especially when Brian Dunigan told a reporter that the family's future plans for the property were confidential. Later that month, Andrew Dunigan was asked if the family would reconsider opening talks with the government. Anything was possible, Dunigan said, "…but at this point I think it is highly doubtful."[22]

The situation hung heavy in the air until the summer of 1999. In June the Dunigan family quietly approached the Council on Environmental Quality at the White House and expressed interest in renewing the talks. This time around, the negotiations were more informal and generated more trust between the participants. Family friend Bill Huey told an Associated Press reporter that he believed that Andy Dunigan and his brothers recognized the strength of their father's desire that the land become public and that realization brought them back to the bargaining table. Huey also counseled Dunigan to stop talking with staff members and go directly to the senators. "Don't talk to the angels, talk to God," Huey said.[23]

In September the USFS made an offer to purchase the Baca Ranch for $101 million, the value specified in the appraisal, and the family accepted. While much work remained to be done in Congress, the Baca acquisition was back on track.[24]

With an agreement in hand, in early November 1999, Senators Domenici and Bingaman introduced Senate Bill 1892, the Valles Caldera Preservation and Federal Land Transaction Facilitation Act, to protect the Baca. A final obstacle was the release of the General Accounting Office (GAO) appraisal in February 2000. The GAO found the ranch to be worth about half of the appraisal submitted by the Dunigans. Several senators balked at the discrepancy, and Domenici and Bingaman called for immediate hearings on the bill. A broad-based group testified in favor of the bill. Jack Craven, Director of Lands for the Forest Service, supported the larger appraised value as a fair market price, noting that the GAO report had failed to look at the recreational and scenic qualities of the land.[25]

The Senate apparently agreed and passed the Valles Caldera Preservation bill in April 2000. One final snag emerged during negotiations on the companion bill in the House of Representatives. Conservative ruling members of the House Subcommittee on National Parks, Forests and Lands held the bill in subcommittee while they attempted to send along to the floor other bills that would be unpalatable to conservationists. New Mexican Representative Heather Wilson of Albuquerque, along with Congressman Tom Udall from northern New Mexico, were able to work a compromise acceptable to all parties. A June 30 deadline came and went, but the family remained sympathetic to the problems the legislation had in the House. Finally, the House vote came on July 12, and the Valles Caldera Preservation Act passed by a 377-45 margin. The $101 million purchase price (minus the previous down payment of $20 million) would come in a lump sum from the Land and Water Conservation Fund.

Representative Wilson, who like the other members of the New Mexico delegation had spent months working on passage of the bill, immediately called the Dunigans to report the successful vote. "I called Andrew (Dunigan) on his cell phone," Wilson said. "This is what his father always wanted. It's taken 30 years to get this done. There is a lot of satisfaction for me and the family."[26]

Passage of the bill received praise from all quarters. At a special White House ceremony held on July 25, 2000, the New Mexico delegation and the Dunigan family celebrated President Clinton's signature on the preservation act. After 100 years of failed attempts, the Baca Location No. 1 and the Valles Caldera were finally returned to the public domain.

The Valles Caldera Preservation Act clearly outlines Congressional expectations for management of the ranch. The bill established the Valles Caldera National Preserve as part of the National Forest System and directs that it be managed by the principle of multiple use. The bill states that "The careful husbandry of the Baca ranch by the current owners, including selective timbering, limited grazing and hunting, and the use of prescribed fire, have preserved a mix of healthy range and timber land with significant species diversity, thereby serving as a model for sustainable land development and use." Management of the property is to continue along the same path, as a working ranch, with public use and reasonable access required.[27]

'Magnificent' Baca Ranch Safeguarded

Headline from the Albuquerque Journal North Edition, *July 26, 2000*

According to the act, management of the Preserve, however, falls not to the USFS but to a third party. The legislation specifically states that the Preserve was established as "a demonstration area for an experimental management regime adapted to this unique property which incorporates elements of public and private administration in order to promote long term financial sustainability consistent with the other purposes...."

To accomplish this, the legislation established the Valles Caldera Trust to oversee the land's administration and management. The Valles Caldera Trust is a wholly owned government corporation. The trust is charged with creating management policies, receiving and collecting public and private funds for the Preserve, and cooperating with nearby pueblos and local governments in issues dealing with the property. The act calls on the trust to pay particular attention to benefits for local communities and small businesses.

A nine-member Board of Trustees presides over the trust; appointments are made by the President of the United States. According to the act; five of the trustees must live in New Mexico, and the board must include members with specific skills in livestock management, sustainable forestry, and fiscal management, as well as members with knowledge of wildlife and fisheries and the cultural and natural history of the region. The board must also include a representative from a nonprofit conservation organization and a representative who is active in state or local government. The superintendent of Bandelier National Monument and the supervisor of the Santa Fe National Forest fill the remaining two seats on the board. Appointed trustees serve for a four-year term, with a maximum of two consecutive terms.

Claw marks from a black bear on an aspen near El Cajete.

Many of the provisions of the law were, and still are, considered controversial. Conservation groups were leery of the stipulation that the Board of Trustees must attempt to make the Preserve financially self-sustaining within 15 years. Many conservationists believed that the emphasis on financial stability conflicts with the more fundamental task of stewardship of the natural and cultural features of the Preserve. Dave Simon, southwest regional director of the National Parks and Conservation Association, testified before a Senate committee that the Presidio Trust model was not suited for natural properties. He feared that the Valles Caldera Trust would make decisions that would compromise the spirit of the legislation. "What appears to be the driving force at the Presidio Trust is the economic self-sufficiency mandate in the authorizing legislation," Simon said. Lawmakers discounted the objections.[28]

Because the management of the Preserve is a grand experiment, the original legislation included a series of special provisions to make clear the rights and standing of other interests in New Mexico. The Secretary of the Department of Agriculture was directed to negotiate with the owners of the minority interests in mineral rights to purchase those rights at fair market value. The only mineral interest right not held by the federal government was the 12.5 percent in the hands of Joab Harrell, who testified before Congress that the geothermal potential of the Preserve was worth pursuing. Because the elk population of the Preserve is an important resource and the potential for high quality angling is well known, the law specifically delegates management responsibility of those resources to the New Mexico Department of Game and Fish. Finally, the law puts about 300 acres of the Preserve under management of nearby Bandelier National Monument for protection of the upper Alamo watershed.

Two additional provisions of the law addressed the concerns of the surrounding pueblos. Santa Clara Pueblo was given the opportunity to acquire the headwaters of Santa Clara Creek found within the boundaries of the Baca Location. Not only did the pueblo wish to protect its water supply, but also its people have strong cultural and religious ties to the entire watershed. Santa Clara purchased 5,046 acres in the northeast corner of the ranch. In addition, many of the Jemez region pueblos want to preserve the cultural significance of Redondo Peak. As a result, the law states that no new roads or structures would be built and no motorized access would be permitted above 10,000 feet on the peak.[29]

Knowing the public's keen desire to explore the property, Congress stipulated that the Board of Trustees, within two years of assuming responsibility for operation of the ranch, develop a management plan and open the ranch to reasonable public access. Explicitly allowed are fee systems for public access, limitations on "the number and types of recreational admissions" based on resources and facilities, and reservation and lottery systems.[30]

Santa Fe National Forest took over temporary management of the new Preserve in late July 2000. USFS officers patrolled the borders, keeping out the curious public, while the federal land management system scrambled to figure out exactly what was supposed to happen with this 88,000-acre experiment.

President Clinton's staff and the New Mexico delegation deliberated far longer than the stated goal of 90 days before announcing the trustees appointed to the initial board. The appointments were made on December 11, 2000. Members of the initial board were William DeBuys, Stephen Stoddard, David Yepa, Robert Armstrong, Karen Durkovich, Palemon Martinez, Thomas Swetnam, Leonard Atencio, and Dennis Vasquez. The board was sworn in on January 12, 2001.

For the members of the Board of Trustees, the adventure—and challenge—of ownership of the Baca Location No. 1 was just beginning.

CHAPTER ELEVEN
2001 TO 2002

BALANCING ACT: WORKING RANCH, PUBLIC PLAYGROUND, AND NATURAL PRESERVE

Northern New Mexico's mountain ranges are draped with dense coats of conifer forest woven with ponderosa pine, Douglas fir, white fir, spruce, and an occasional swatch of aspen. In the Jemez Mountains, surprisingly extensive grasslands push this bold green covering out of the valleys and hold it at bay on the slopes. Particularly on cloudless summer mornings, an intricate quilt of pastel green hues in the grasslands can stop visitors dead in their tracks and intice them to linger over the subtle interplay of colors. Few who gaze across the *valles* are completely immune to the temptation to tramp across the fields, but private ownership has barred entry to the Baca Ranch for decades. Rare is a hiker, skier, or mountain biker who hasn't lusted to feel the bumps of the Valles Caldera beneath boot, board, or tire. More than a few recreationists have sneaked across the fence and entered the hallowed ground. Be it skiing to a hot spring under a full moon, a commando climb up one of the peaks, or casting a line into the East Fork of the Jemez River below the Valle Grande, most locals have a tale of illegal entry onto the Baca Ranch.

In July 2000 *Los Valles* and the surrounding mountains came under federal ownership as the Valles Caldera National Preserve. An anxious public expected immediate, legal, and unlimited access; what the people got was a closure order for the entire property, and stricter enforcement of the boundary line than ever before. The Preserve entered the uncharted waters of a publicly owned natural area managed by a trust of the federal government. There was no map, no compass, no guiding stars, and at first not even a captain to sail this misfit ship. The Preserve could only drift until the crew sorted out the meaning of the law that set the ship in motion.

The presidential appointment of seven trustees was a start. Still dependent on the USFS to provide even the basic protective and operational services, the new management of the Preserve started to sift through the unique set of stipulations set up by Congress to operate the property as a working ranch. The complex issues of the untried management system were difficult to resolve.

Two years after the sale to the government, the former ranch remained closed to the public.

It wasn't for lack of trying. In February 2001 the Board of Trustees held the first of a long string of public meetings. The trust employed professional facilitators at these "listening sessions" to help elicit and organize input from the public. The trustees always got an earful, especially when a session took place at recreationally oriented Los Alamos. More than 150 people jammed the meeting room at the Betty Ehart Senior Center and about 40 spoke, calling for access for skiing, hiking, sensible grazing and logging, and the economic boost of a visitor center in town. Others spoke passionately for the idea of keeping the ranch closed to public access.[1]

With enough ideas to fill the Valle Grande, the board started work on a comprehensive management plan. Brush fires kept diverting their attention to a far narrower focus: a water system, paying their staff from the proper fund, petitioning Congress for an allocation to keep the Preserve afloat during its transition period, and other issues. The trustees, led by Chairman William DeBuys, wanted a management tool from which to sail. To provide direction for the trust, on December 13, 2001, the Board of Trustees adopted ten management principles.

Management Principles of the Valles Caldera Trust

1. We will administer the Preserve with the long term in mind, directing our efforts toward the benefit of future generations.

2. Recognizing that the Preserve possesses a rich sense of place and qualities not to be found anywhere else, we commit ourselves to the protection of its ecological, cultural, and aesthetic integrity.

3. We will strive to achieve a high level of integrity in our stewardship of the lands, programs and other assets in our care. This includes adopting an ethic of financial thrift and discipline and exercising good business sense.

4. We will exercise restraint in the implementation of all programs, basing them on sound science and adjusting them consistent with the principles of adaptive management.

5. Recognizing the unique heritage of northern New Mexico's traditional cultures, we will be a good neighbor to surrounding communities, striving to avoid negative impacts from Preserve activities and to generate positive impacts.

6. Recognizing the religious significance of the Preserve to Native Americans, the Trust bears a special responsibility to accommodate the religious practices of nearby tribes and pueblos, and to protect sites of special significance.

7. Recognizing the importance of clear and open communication, we commit ourselves to maintaining a productive dialogue with those who would advance the purposes of the Preserve and, where appropriate, to developing partnerships with them.

8. Recognizing that the Preserve is part of a larger ecological whole, we will cooperate with adjacent landowners and managers to achieve a healthy regional ecosystem.

9. Recognizing the great potential of the Preserve for learning and inspiration, we will strive to integrate opportunities for research, reflection and education in the programs of the Preserve.

10. In providing opportunities to the public, we will emphasize quality of experience over quantity of experiences. In doing so, while we reserve the right to limit participation or to maximize revenue in certain instances, we commit ourselves to providing fair and affordable access for all permitted activities.[2]

Choosing to err on the side of caution, the board moved slowly in allowing public access to the property. In their management principles, the trustees affirmed their belief in using sound science to make decisions. The trustees wanted baseline data for natural and cultural resources on which to base monitoring of the impacts of the various activities planned for visitors to the Preserve. By monitoring impacts, the board felt they could respond to problem areas, re-assess their management strategies, and implement new ideas to correct problems. As a result of the emphasis on science, the Preserve was a magnet that drew researchers and in the first two years, scientists from around the West donated their services in studying flora, bats, breeding birds, skinks, endangered species, soils, and geology on the property. The trustees expanded their staff to include a scientist to develop and oversee a research plan.

Central to management of the Preserve was the issue of the impacts of grazing both by cattle and elk. To that end, the Preserve staff quickly established a long-term research project to document the effects of grazing on the riparian areas in the grassland valleys. Working sometimes in the midst of a grazing cattle herd, workers began construction of six paired exclosures. One in each of the major valleys, each exclosure has two cells. A four-foot fence, designed to keep cattle out but allow elk to enter, surrounds one cell; the other cell fences out all grazing ungulates with eight-foot high wire. The research plan was to isolate the effects on grasses, shrubs, and native plants by grazing elk and cattle.

Aside from two weekends of short walking tours in September 2001, public use of the property began on August 19, 2002. Strung out along the twisting entrance road to the Preserve, a convoy of vehicles kicked up plumes of dust. Pickups lugged overloaded stock trailers, each taller and longer than the trucks themselves. Under an unbroken dome of blue, their common destination—the Black Corrals—was the only man-made object visible in the bottom of the Valle Grande. As they had for almost two hundred years, the lush grasslands of the Valle Grande and its neighboring *valles* sang a powerful siren song to the stockmen of the region.[3]

At the corrals about a dozen trustees, staff, and other onlookers gathered to witness the unloading of the first trailer. Under the watchful eye of Ranch Foreman Randy McKee, Gilbert Gonzales pushed a reluctant black cow off the flatbed, its hooves thudding as they hit the ground. The owner encouraged two more cows to drop off the trailer, and they needed no additional prodding to move into the holding pen where thick forage covered the ground. For the first time under federal ownership, cattle trod on the former Baca Ranch.

From the center of the Valle Grande, the world is a sea of grass rippling off to the horizon. A few hundred yards south, Cerro La Jara—appropriately called The Island by five generations of sheepherders and cowboys—brakes the rhythm of the rolling prairie. The traditional name originated on summer mornings that were a jarring contrast to this one. When enough moisture hangs in the air overnight, morning presents a *valle* filled with a ground-hugging, thick cloud. The surrounding hills become the rim of a green bowl that holds a fog soup. Only The Island punches through the top of the fog, an isolated rock pile drifting on the white sea.

Like most of the post-World War II structures on the Preserve, the Black Corrals were built for cattle. A series of interlocking pens, the rusted steel bars seem more like a child's puzzle than a place to sort livestock. A maze of fences broken by double-wide gates encloses a quarter acre of pasture. In the middle of the labyrinth sit the livestock scales, their protective wooden shed weathered to a comfortable gray. The previous ranch owners, the Dunigan family, found it difficult to make a profit on grazing leases even on the rich meadows of *Los Valles* until ranch manager Danny Stevens started charging grazing fees based on weight gain instead of simple head counts. It's never been easy for stockmen to make a living at high elevations.

Yet on this summer morning cattlemen stood eager to watch the Preserve staff release their stock from the pens and into the

Interest in the Preserve has always been high. In September 2001, the Valles Caldera Board of Trustees opened the Preserve for two weekends of guided tours. The phone lines for reservations received 50,000 calls the first day for the 1,500 tour slots.

tan grasslands of the *valle*. They arrived hours before the scheduled time, impatient to have their cow-and-calf units enjoy 43 days
of grazing on the Preserve. "The grass in the pen beats anything
these cows have seen all summer," said one of the ranchers,
watching a half-starved cow with hipbones barely hidden by its
brown hide as it ripped grass from the ground.

The presence of loudly chewing cows and calves was the
result of a fiercely contested discussion. During the drought-
plagued summer of 2002, rangelands throughout northern New
Mexico were appallingly barren. An inspection by a ranking USFS
official resulted in a decree for local ranchers to remove their
stock from grazing allotments on the Santa Fe National Forest.

Threatened
with the loss of
at least part of
their livelihood,
ranchers eyed
the higher,
greener mead-
ows in the
Valles Caldera
National Pre-
serve. Required
by law to be a
working ranch,
the Preserve
management
felt obligated to
consider
grazing leases
before a com-
plete manage-
ment plan was
in place.

*Randy McKee
watches as the first
cattle on the Valles
Caldera National
Preserve drop from
the stock trailer.*

At a public meeting of the Valles Caldera Board of Trustees
in Los Alamos, tempers flared. Cattlemen angrily demanded
access to the grasslands on the Preserve, claiming that their
lifestyle and economic security were threatened. Recreationists
cried foul, scandalized that the trampling hooves of grazing
ungulates would set foot on the Preserve before the soles of
hikers' boots. Fishermen argued that undercut banks, the perfect
hiding spots for large trout, would be destroyed. For the nine-
member Board of Trustees, no solution would be popular with all
its constituents, not even its final decision to allow grazing, but at
a far lower level than requested by the stockmen.

It was the unique management system of the Preserve that
permitted such a quick response to the cry for cattle in the
grasslands. Without all the levels of bureaucracy that are atten-

dant to the other federal lands, the Board of Trustees could expedite a decision—within the constraints of environmental and cultural protection laws. Not all the board was comfortable with implementing a hasty grazing program, but the summer's events demonstrated the difficulties the board would face.

Watching the mixed herds of Black Angus, Herefords, and the mutts of the cow world mill around the holding pen, the immensity of the task faced by the initial trustees was as difficult to avoid as stepping in a fresh cow pie. With a culturally and economically diverse New Mexican constituency, the trustees could not help but anger some segment of the public. Grazing was a sensitive hot button. The suggestion had been made in a letter to the editor of the *Los Alamos Monitor* that the trustees be barbecued for their decision to put cows in the Valle Grande. And grazing was only one of dozens of issues they stared down each time they peered at the future of the Preserve. Public access. Protection of cultural sites. Road improvements. Stabilization of historic buildings. Wildfire threat. Thinning operations. Running an 88,000-acre ranch with a staff of six employees. Funding for environmental assessments. A rim trail. All these demands, and there wasn't even potable water in the Preserve headquarters area!

It was suddenly so easy. After decades of being fenced out of the Baca Ranch, an eager group of a dozen hikers simply walked across the boundary line as the gate at the foot of Rabbit Mountain slowly swung open. The members of this group, crossing the fenceline on August 30, 2002, were the first-ever (legal) hikers on the Valles Caldera National Preserve.

The group was comprised mostly of locals who for years had yearned to set foot on the Baca Ranch. All smiles, the group climbed an old logging road for a few minutes before turning around and soaking in their first view of the Valle Grande from a place other than along the highway. Five minutes of walking gave an entirely different perspective on the familiar scene. With the road hidden beneath a swale, the rest of the world seemed to have melted away. The forested bowl of the Valle Grande appeared even larger than it did from the paved road.

The group ambled past chest-high ponderosa pine stumps, sawed by hand more than 50 years before. Aspens along the route were carved with names of sheepherders who camped there even before the parents of the hikers had been born. Elk bones disturbed by foraging coyotes were scattered across an aspen-lined meadow. After two hours of steady climbing through thick conifer forest, the group emerged onto a jumble of rocks on the ridgeline north of Rabbit Mountain. Directly below, the Valle Grande spread from horizon to horizon. For many in the group, it was a dream come true.

But it was not an ordinary hiking experience: not only was the destination new, but so were the rules. The Board of Trustees dictated special conditions for the first hikers in the Preserve. Because the area has no parking lot, visitors were shuttled from Los Alamos. With no hard data on impacts of dispersed recreation, trained guides accompanied all visitors. Transportation, guides, and a firm idea of how they expected the hikes to be operated required the trustees to enter a contract with a local tour business. Such arrangements cost money, and each of the hikers, as well as others to follow, paid $45 apiece to go on a four-hour tour.

Following the familiar pattern, the organization of the hiking tours set off another storm of controversy for the Board of Trustees. The opinion pages of area newspapers were filled with vindictive letters about "a playground for the rich."

Hiking tours operated by a private company opened public access to the Valles Caldera National Preserve in August 2002.

Placards stapled to the Preserve's interpretive signs along the highway proclaimed the Valle Grande as "Pete's Feedlot," a reference to New Mexico's Senator Pete Dominici, who many perceived as a pivotal player in setting up how the Preserve is managed. "Access for Cows, $1.50 for six weeks; Access for People, $10 an hour."

But cows before people wasn't such a stretch. For more than 150 years the property had been a working ranch. Scattered about its 88,000 acres are corrals, holding pens, tack shacks, barns, stables, and enough fence to enclose the entire state. Never has there been a need for recreation facilities—not even the most basic parking lots, bathrooms, or a place to find a drink of water.

The contrasting deep-throated moans of cattle and pleading cries of the calves filled the warming August air. When the pens were loaded with about 50 head, Randy McKee and one of the

hired hands strode over to their horses. Each rider swung a chap-
covered leg over his horse's rump, swept up the reins, and eased
his horse into the corral. Winding through the maze of fence and
threading through the herd, the ranch hand stopped at the gate
into the pasture. With no fanfare, he reached down and flipped up
the clasp. The gate swung open, and immediately the cattle
followed the cowboy to the wide-open grasslands. Before taking a
dozen steps, most of the cows stopped to loudly munch the fresh
grass. McKee urged the last of the line through the gate, and with
the ease of one who has spent years on horseback behind a mob
of cows, he slid the herd away from the corrals.

Cattle were back in the pastures grazed for more than a
century. Caught up in the moment, one of the observers cried,
"The Baca lives!"

If Randy McKee was excited to be back on the range he rode
for a nearly a decade, it didn't show. He maintained a serene
cowboy manner as he swung his horse easily back and forth
behind the herd, gently nudging them further out into the pasture.
About 700 cows spent the waning days of summer munching
fescues, muhlys, and other range grasses on the Valle Grande and
Valle Jaramillo. McKee and his riders rotated the herds almost
daily, keeping the cattle from grazing any single pasture for too
long.

Born out of controversy as settlement for the conflicting
land claims of the Cabeza de Baca family and the community of
Las Vegas, the Baca Location No. 1 is likely to remain close to its
contentious roots. The Valles Caldera National Preserve is billed
as a great experiment in federal land management. The gates are
wide open for spirited arguments from those with conflicting
viewpoints on cattle grazing, elk hunting, public access, and
construction of visitor facilities. The bowl-shaped caldera, no
longer isolated, will be the focus of intense scrutiny as Congress,
resource managers nationwide, and the surrounding communities
watch as the continuing story of land use of the caldera unfolds.

NOTES

Chapter 1: Big Bangs: The Volcanic History of the Valles Caldera

[1] Stephen Self, Grant Heiken, Martha L. Sykes, Kenneth Wohletz, Richard V. Fisher, and David P. Dethier, *Field Excursions to the Jemez Mountains, New Mexico*, Socorro: New Mexico Bureau of Mines and Mineral Resources, Bulletin 134, 1996. This excellent summary of Jemez Mountain geology represents more than 50 years of field studies in the Jemez range. For a visualization of the complexities of the layer-cake mountains, look at R. L. Smith, R. A. Bailey, and C. S. Ross, *Geologic Map of the Jemez Mountains, New Mexico*, U.S. Geological Survey Miscellaneous Geologic Investigations Map I-571, 1976. Additional information on the geology of the region was obtained from March to December 2002 through conversations with Grant Heiken, Fraser Goff, and Jamie Gardner.

[2] Fraser Goff, and Jamie N. Gardner, "Valles Caldera Region, New Mexico, and the Emerging Continental Scientific Drilling Program," *Journal of Geophysical Research*, vol. 93, no. B6, June 10, 1988, p.559; Clarence S. Ross and Robert L. Smith, *Ash-Flow Tuffs: Their Origin, Geologic Relations, and Identification*, United States Geological Survey Professional Paper 366, 1960, reprinted by the New Mexico Geological Society, Socorro, New Mexico, 1980.

[3] Fraser Goff, "Geothermal Potential of Valles Caldera, New Mexico," *Geo-Heat Center Quarterly Bulletin*, vol. 23, no. 4, Klamath Falls: Oregon Institute of Technology, 2002, p. 10.

Chapter 2: Beginnings: The Pueblo People and the Spanish Era

[1] Joe S. Sando, *Nee Hemish: A History of Jemez Pueblo*, Albuquerque: University of New Mexico Press, 1982, pp. 4-11.

[2] Peter Pino, lecture at the University of New Mexico–Los Alamos, March 5, 2002. Used with permission.

[3] James L. Moore, Bradley J. Vierra, Gale M. McPherson, and Mark E. Harlan, *An Investigation into High Altitude Adaptations: The Baca Geothermal Project*, Albuquerque: Office of Contract Archeology, University of New Mexico, 1978, pp. 92-93.

[4] Anastasia Steffen, interview with the author, May 10, 2002.

[5] Sando, pp. 15-16; Lois Vermilya Weslowski, "Native American Land Use Along Redondo Creek," in *High Altitude Adaptations along Redondo Creek: The Baca Geothermal Anthropological Project*, Albuquerque: Office of Contract Archeology, University of New Mexico, 1981, p. 108.

[6] Interview with Anastasia Steffen.

[7] Rory Gauthier, personal communication, September 11, 2001.

[8] Lansing B. Bloom, "The West Jemez Cultural Area," *New Mexico Historical Review*, vol. 21, p. 123. Reprinted from *El Palacio*, January 15, 1922.

[9] Bernardo Miera y Pacheco, *Plano de la Provincia Interna de el Nuebo Mexico, que hizo por mandado de el Tnte. Coronel de Caballeria, Gobernador y Comte,* 1779. Located in the Map Room at the History Library, Museum of New Mexico, Santa Fe, New Mexico. Valle de los Bacas may have been a reference to bison, but researchers have not yet found direct evidence that bison ranged into the Valles Caldera.

[10] Weslowski, p. 115; Nancy J. Atkins, "Traditional Use Areas in New Mexico," *Archaeology Notes* No. 141, Santa Fe: Museum of New Mexico, Office of Archaeological Studies, 1993, pp. 70-186.

Chapter 3: American Military Actions on the Jemez Frontier

[1] Robert W. Frazer, *Forts and Supplies: The Role of the Army in the Economy of the Southwest, 1846-1861*, Albuquerque: University of New Mexico Press, 1983, p. 50.

[2] Letter from Robert Nesbit and Hiram Parker to Col. John Munroe, as cited in Frank McNitt, *Navajo Wars: Military Campaigns, Slave Raids and Reprisals*, Albuquerque: University of New Mexico Press, 1972, pp. 185-186; Letter from Dick Boyd to Homer Pickens, November 16, 1964, Peggy Pond Church Collection, Los Alamos Historical Society Archives. Boyd was able to trace the "military road" when he arrived on the Pajarito Plateau in the 1910s. He described a steep section of the road that topped one of the ridges as a "wampus cat."

[3] McNitt, pp. 185-186. Nesbit worked many shady deals with Army Quartermaster Alexander W. Reynolds that placed them among the wealthiest men in the Territory. See Weymouth T. Jordan, Jr., John D. Chapla, and Shan C. Sutton, " 'Notorious as the Noonday Sun': Capt. Alexander Welch Reynolds and the New Mexico Territory, 1849-1859," *New Mexico Historical Review*, vol. 75, 2000, pp. 465, 494.

[4] Boyd letter to Pickens.

[5] Dan Scurlock, "Euro-American History of the Study Area," in *High Altitude Adaptations along Redondo Creek: The Baca Geothermal Anthropological Project,*

Albuquerque: Office of Contract Archeology, University of New Mexico, 1981, p. 137. Scurlock was the first to look at the history of the Baca Location No. 1.

[6] William A. Keleher, *Turmoil in New Mexico*, Albuquerque: University of New Mexico Press, 1982, p. 314, reprinted from Rydal Press in Santa Fe, 1952.

[7] "Volcanic Crater World's Largest," *Los Alamos Scientific Laboratory Community News*, July 16, 1959, pp. 4-5.

Chapter 4: The Luis Maria Cabeza de Baca Land Grant

[1] J. J. Bowden, "Private Land Claims in the Southwest," Master's Thesis, Houston, Texas, 1969, vol. 3, p. 793.

[2] George C de Baca, *A Genealogical Record of the Cabeza de Baca Family of New Mexico*, self-published, 1999, pp. 11-12.

[3] C de Baca, p. 69.

[4] Malcolm Ebright, *Land Grants and Lawsuits in Northern New Mexico*, Albuquerque: University of New Mexico Press, 1994, pp. 174-175.

[5] John O. Baxter, *Las Carneradas: Sheep Trade in New Mexico 1700-1860*, Albuquerque: University of New Mexico Press, 1987, p. 20.

[6] Bowden, p. 794.

[7] Josiah Gregg, *Commerce on the Prairies*, edited by Max L. Moorhead, Norman: University of Oklahoma Press, 1954, p. 76-77.

[8] David J. Weber, *The Taos Trappers: The Fur Trade in the Far Southwest, 1540-1846*, Norman: University of Oklahoma Press, 1971, p. 129; Robert Glass Cleland, *This Reckless Breed of Men· Trappers and Fur Traders of the Southwest*, Lincoln: University of Nebraska Press, 1992, p. 219, reprinted from 1950 edition; Records of the Surveyor General, New Mexico, Luis Maria Cabeza de Baca Grant, File No. 103, Spanish Archives of New Mexico I, New Mexico State Records Center and Archives, Santa Fe, New Mexico.

[9] Ebright, pp. 175-178; Clark S. Knowlton, "The Town of Las Vegas Community Land Grant: An Anglo American Coup D'Etat," in *Spanish and American Land Grants in New Mexico and Colorado*, edited by John R. and Christine M. Van Ness, Manhattan, Kansas: Sunflower University Press, 1988; Milton W. Callon, *Las Vegas, New Mexico...The Town that Wouldn't Gamble*, Las Vegas, N.M.: Las Vegas Publishing Co., 1962.

[10] Ebright, pp. 179-181.

[11] House of Representatives Executive Document No. 14, 36th Congress, First Session, 37, 1860, pp. 40-42, as cited in Bowden, p. 797.

[12] David Remley, *Bell Ranch: Cattle Ranching in the Southwest, 1824-1947*, Albuquerque: University of New Mexico Press, 1993, pp. 40-46.

[13] Records of Private Land Claims Adjudicated by the U. S. Surveyor General, Roll 31, Spanish Archives of New Mexico I, New Mexico State Records Center and Archives, Santa Fe, New Mexico.

[14] Brief of the Claimants by Watts and Jackson, Attorneys, The Baca Grant, Records of Private Land Claims Adjudicated by the U. S. Surveyor General, Roll 31, Spanish Archives of New Mexico I, New Mexico State Records Center and Archives, Santa Fe, New Mexico.

[15] Records of the 36th Congress, First Session, June 1860, U. S. Public Law 167, "An Act to Confirm Certain Private Land Claims in the Territory of New Mexico."

[16] Angelico Chavez, *Origins of New Mexico Families: A Genealogy of the Spanish Colonial Period*, Santa Fe: Museum of New Mexico Press, 1992, p. 153.

[17] Jay J. Wagoner, *Early Arizona: Prehistory to Civil War*, Tucson: University of Arizona Press, 1975, pp. 200-210; Bowden, pp. 798-808. Bowden records that Baca Location No. 5 was originally located along the Pecos River at Bosque Redondo. Indian hostilities in the area prevented the survey of the boundaries, and the family (or more likely John Watts) requested permission to withdraw the selection and relocate it in Yavapai County, Arizona.

[18] Records of Private Land Claims Adjudicated by the U. S. Surveyor General, Roll 31, Spanish Archives of New Mexico I, New Mexico State Records Center and Archives, Santa Fe, New Mexico.

[19] Letter from W. W. Gunter to Rush Spencer, Territorial Archives of New Mexico, Land Grant Records, Roll 14, Spanish Archives of New Mexico I, New Mexico State Records Center and Archives, Santa Fe, New Mexico; Sawyer and McBroom. "Field Notes of the Survey of the Baca Location No. One, in New Mexico, being a Grant made to the heirs of Luis Maria Baca by act of Congress approved June 21, 1860," General Land Office Records, Bureau of Land Management Archives, Santa Fe, New Mexico.

[20] Adolph Bandelier, *Final Report of Investigations Among the Indians of the Southwestern United States, carried on mainly in the years from 1880 to 1885*, Cambridge, 1892, pp. 200. In his journal, Bandelier noted that there were river otters in the Valle Grande.

[21] The 1909 map drawn by L. D. W. Shelton shows an "old cabin" in the Valle Toledo. At present, the ruins of a small cabin lie in approximately the same location. Four aspens with a diameter of more than 12 inches grow within the cabin walls. Tree ring analysis may show that this is indeed the "old cabin."

[22] Lynn I. Perrigo, *Hispanos: Historic Leaders in New Mexico*, Santa Fe: Sunstone Press, 1985, p. 22.

[23] For example the will of Jose Perea gives his "undivided 13/168 interest in the Baca Location No. 1" to his son.

[24] Victor Westphall, *Thomas Benton Catron and His Era*, Tucson: University of Arizona Press, 1973, pp. 71-72; Records of the Bernalillo County Clerk's Office, 1876-1903, New Mexico State Records Center and Archives, Santa Fe, New Mexico.

[25] Miguel Antonio Otero, *My Life on the Frontier, 1864 to 1882*, New York: The Press of the Pioneers, 1935; Records of the Bernalillo County Clerk's Office, 1876-1903, New Mexico State Records Center and Archives, Santa Fe, New Mexico.

[26] Joel Parker Whitney vs. Mariano S. Otero et al. (Civil Case No. 3632), Records of the United States Territorial and New Mexico District Courts for Bernalillo County, New Mexico State Records Center and Archives, Santa Fe, New Mexico. The sale agreement between James Whitney and Maria Gertrudis Cabeza de Baca is part of the court records and is listed as Exhibit N.

[27] Whitney vs. Otero et al., petition for partition of the Baca Location No. 1, 1893.

[28] Otero, pp. 97-108; Erna Fergusson, *Murder and Mystery in New Mexico*, Santa Fe: The Lightning Tree, reprint of 1948 edition by Merle Armitage, pp. 33-48; Charles Pope, "The Estancia Springs Tragedy," *New Mexico Historical Review*, vol. 20, 1945, pp. 189-206.

[29] Whitney vs. Otero et al., exceptions to master's reports by Thomas Catron and Mariano Otero, probably 1897.

[30] Whitney vs. Otero et al., commissioners' report, December 4, 1898.

[31] Whitney vs. Otero et al., report on sale of Baca Location No. 1, Harry F. Lee, 1899.

[32] Records of the Bernalillo County Assessosr's Office, 1876-1903, New Mexico State Records Center and Archives, Santa Fe, New Mexico.

Chapter 5: Changing Hands: Sulfur, Sheep, Timber, and Speculation

[1] Records of the Bernalillo County Assessor's Office, 1876-1903, New Mexico State Records Center and Archives, Santa Fe, New Mexico.

[2] W. K. Summers, *Catalog of Thermal Waters in New Mexico*, Socorro: New Mexico Bureau of Mines and Mineral Resources, 1976, p. 32-34.

[3] The exact route of Otero's road has not been completely traced on the ground. The 1892 topographic map, *Jemez Sheet*, by the United States Geologic Survey shows much of the route of Otero's road in place. Shelton's 1909 map of the Baca Location illustrates what is assumed to be the completed route.

[4] *Santa Fe Daily New Mexican*, June 21, 1902; July 2, 1902; July 30, 1902.

[5] Dan Scurlock, "Euro-American History of the Study Area," in *High Altitude Adaptations along Redondo Creek: The Baca Geothermal Anthropological Project*, Albuquerque: Office of Contract Archeology, University of New Mexico, 1981, p. 141; G. R. Mansfield, "Sulphur in Jemez Canyon, Sandoval County," United States Geological Survey, *Mineral Resources*, 1918, p. 367.

[6] Records of the Bernalillo County Assessor's Office, 1876-1903, New Mexico State Records Center and Archives, Santa Fe, New Mexico.

[7] *Diary of Eurl G. Sparks and Harry L. Sparks: Their Trip from Pagosa Springs, Colorado to Phoenix, Arizona and Return, October 1902 to April 1903*, unpublished manuscript, used with permission of John Sparks; Lorin W. Brown, *Hispano Folklife of New Mexico: The Lorin W. Brown Federal Writers' Project Manuscripts*, Albuquerque: University of New Mexico Press, 1978, p. 166. Brown's work holds a detailed description of the camp life of Basilico Garduño, who as a young man worked for Mariano Otero.

[8] Olen E. Leonard, *The Role of the Land Grant in the Social Organization and Social Processes of a Spanish-American Village in New Mexico*, Albuquerque: Calvin Horn, 1970.

[9] Letter from Napoleon Laughlin to L. W. Dennis, August 14, 1907, Napoleon B. Laughlin Papers, New Mexico State Records Center and Archives, Santa Fe, New Mexico.

[10] Scurlock, p. 141.

[11] William DeBuys, *Jemez Mountain Field Notes of Vernon O. Bailey*, 1906, unpublished manuscript based on archival material at the Smithsonian Institution. Used with permission of William DeBuys, who transcribed Bailey's field notes.

[12] Records of the Sandoval County Tax Assessor's Office, 1903-1912, New Mexico State Records Center and Archives, Santa Fe, New Mexico; L. D. W. Shelton, *Map of the Baca Location No. 1, New Mexico*, 1909. Shelton's map of the Baca Location No. 1 shows two structures on the banks of La Jara Creek. Biologist Vernon Bailey rode through the Valle Toledo in September 1906 and reported "No one lives in it." That same year a timber cruiser reported that there was "...not a squatter or homestead on the tract." Thus Otero most likely built this cabin and commissary in either 1907 or 1908.

[13] Records of the Sandoval County Clerk's Office, 1903-1940, Deed of Record Book 5, p. 191; letter from Otto Hake to Mary Ann Bond Bunten, undated, in the private collection of the Bond family.

[14] Willard S. Hopewell Papers, Center for Southwest Research, General Library, University of New Mexico; 1930 Federal Census, Warren County, Pennsylvania.[15] From Shelton's map.

[16] Bandelier, 1892, pp. 200-201.

[17] Scurlock, p. 142.

[18] Letter from Fred Dennett, Commissioner of the General Land Office, to Charles T. Hendler, Attorney for Redondo Development Company, July 5, 1912, Records of Private Land Claims Adjudicated by the U.S. Surveyor General, Roll 31, Spanish Archives of New Mexico I, New Mexico State Records Center and Archives, Santa Fe, New Mexico.

[19] *Ibid.*

[20] William B. Douglas, *Field Notes of the Restorative Survey of the Baca Location No. 1, 1912*, General Land Office Records, Bureau of Land Management Archives, Santa Fe, New Mexico.

[21] Records of the Circuit Court of Appeals, Eighth Circuit, Case 254 F. 656, United States V. Redondo Development Company, New Mexico State Supreme Court Library, Santa Fe, New Mexico; "Redondo Co. Wins Suit," *Santa Fe New Mexican*, November 26, 1918, p. 5.

[22] L. A. Osterhoudt, W. V. Hall, and Charles W. Devendorf, *Field Notes of the Independent Resurvey of the Boundaries of the Baca Location No. 1, Grant, 1920-1921*, General Land Office Records, Bureau of Land Management Archives, Santa Fe, New Mexico.

[23] George M. White, "This Is My Life," unpublished manuscript, 1958, Los Alamos Historical Society Archives. Used with permission of Jim and Linda Goforth.

[24] Record of Homestead Entry No. 261, General Land Office Records, Bureau of Land Management Archives, Santa Fe, New Mexico.

[25] White manuscript; Crop and Residence Report for H. E. No. 023824, United States Forest Service, Santa Fe National Forest Surveyor's Office, 1915 to 1917. Chris Chavez, a surveyor with the Santa Fe National Forest, provided the homestead reports filed by Fred Plomteaux.

[26] Report on Homestead Claim H. E. 023824, Fred Plomteaux to Santa Fe National Forest, 1919. General Land Office Records, Bureau of Land Management Archives, Santa Fe.

[27] Records of the Sandoval County Clerk's Office, Deed of Record Book 2, p. 439, and Miscellaneous Record Book 1, p. 199.

Chapter 6: The Bond Family in the Valle Grande

[1] Craig D. Allen, *Changes in the Landscape of the Jemez Mountains, New Mexico*, Ph.D. dissertation, University of California, Berkeley1989.

[2] "Frank Bond, Necrology," *New Mexico Historical Review*, vol. 20, 1945, pp. 271-272.

[3] Letter from Frank Bond to Edward Wetmore, November 10, 1916, Frank Bond & Son Records, Center for Southwest Research, General Library, University of New Mexico, vol. 41, p. 349.

[4] Letter from Frank Bond to Edward Wetmore, February 16, 1917, Frank Bond & Son Records, Center for Southwest Research, General Library, University of New Mexico, vol. 41, p. 642.

[5] Quemado Sheep Company, ledger, 1918-1919, Frank Bond & Son Records, Center for Southwest Research, General Library, University of New Mexico, vol. 8.

[6] Frank Bond letters to Edward Wetmore, June 22, 1917 and July 20, 1917, Frank Bond & Son Records, Center for Southwest Research, General Library, University of New Mexico, vol. 96, pp. 216, 557.

[7] Baca Location, 1918, Frank Bond & Son Records, Center for Southwest Research, General Library, University of New Mexico, vol. 170.

[8] Letter from Frank Bond to Edward Wetmore, March 20, 1918, Frank Bond & Son Records, Center for Southwest Research, General Library, University of New Mexico, vol. 95.

[9] "Another Big Land Sale," *Santa Fe New Mexican*, December 17, 1918.

[10] Bond Company, Current Ledger No. 1, 1912-1925, Frank Bond & Son Records, Center for Southwest Research, General Library, University of New Mexico, vol. 31; Bernalillo County Clerk's Office, Miscellaneous Records Book 2, p. 31.

[11] Baca Location, 1918, Frank Bond & Son Records, Center for Southwest Research, General Library, University of New Mexico, vol. 170.

[12] Charles H. Corlett, *Cowboy Pete*, Santa Fe: Sunstone Press, 1974.

[13] James L. Moore, Bradley J. Vierra, Gale M. McPherson and Mark E. Harlan, *An Investigation into High Altitude Adaptations: The Baca Geothermal Project*, Albuquerque: Office of Contract Archeology, University of New Mexico, 1978, p. 94. The fall burning of pastures by herders presents interesting questions concerning forest densities. See Craig Allen, "Lots of Lightning and Plenty of People," in *Fire, Native Peoples, and the Natural Landscape*, edited by Thomas R. Vale, Washington, D. C.: Island Press, 2002, pp. 170-177.

[14] Dan Scurlock, "Euro-American History of the Study Area," in *High Altitude Adaptations along Redondo Creek: The Baca Geothermal Anthropological Project*, Albuquerque: Office of Contract Archeology, University of New Mexico, 1981, p. 144. Scurlock interviewed former residents of the area.

[15] Edward Norris Wentworth, *America's Sheep Trails*, Ames: Iowa State College Press, 1948.

[16] James B. DeKorne, *Aspen Art in the New Mexico Highlands*, Santa Fe: Museum of New Mexico Press, 1970, pp. 10-12.

[17] Surveys by the author, summer 2002. David Hayes of Bandelier National Monument located the 1875 carving along the Valle Santa Rosa.

[18] William DeBuys, personal communication. DeBuys knows of a similar place in the Sangre de Cristo Mountains that is locally called *La Iglesia*, "the church."

[19] William A. Douglass, *Basque Sheepherders of the American West: A Photographic Documentary*, Reno: University of Nevada Press, 1985, pp. 80-81.

[20] Frank Bond, "The Bond Family and the Baca Location," lecture to the Los Alamos Historical Society, May 15, 1991. Audiotape at the Los Alamos Historical Society Archives.

[21] *Ibid*.

[22] John O. Baxter, *Las Carneradas: Sheep Trade in New Mexico 1700-1860*, Albuquerque: University of New Mexico Press, 1987, pp. 28-30.

23 Contract between Jose Antonio Montoya and Vincente Armijo, 1829, as cited in DeKorne, pp. 9-10.

24 Daniel T. Kelly (with Beatrice Chauvenet), *The Buffalo Head: A Century of Merchantile Pioneering in the Southwest*, Santa Fe: Vergara Publishing Company, 1972, pp. 190-191.

25 Hal K. Rothman, *On Rim and Ridges: The Los Alamos Area since 1880*, Lincoln: University of Nebraska Press, 1997. Rothman paints a dark picture of the *partido* system under Bond, citing some cutthroat business practices that made it nearly impossible to escape debt under a company contract.

26 "Frank Bond Dies, Pioneer Sheep and Business Man," *Albuquerque Journal*, June 22, 1945.

27 "Frank Bond, Necrology," *New Mexico Historical Review*, vol. 20, 1945, pp. 271-272.

28 Dan Bunten, interview by the author, November 20, 2002.

29 Lois Vermilya Weslowski, "Native American Land Use Along Redondo Creek," in *High Altitude Adaptations along Redondo Creek: The Baca Geothermal Anthropological Project*, Albuquerque: Office of Contract Archeology, University of New Mexico, 1981, p. 115.

30 Los Alamos Ranch School, 1934 Brochure, Ranch School Collection, Los Alamos Historical Society Archives.

31 "Notes for Docents, Baca Location Tours," unpublished notes from interviews with Baca Ranch staff, Los Alamos Historical Society, 1991, Los Alamos Historical Society Archives.

32 Mary Ann Bond Bunten, interview by the author, November 20, 2002. The cabin built for Sam and Bertilla Hill was later used as a bunkhouse, and then a morning gathering point for ranch hands. For convenience, the Dunigan family gave names to the cabins, and called this one the Greer Cabin. It was named for the large Greer family, friends of the Dunigans who lived in Santa Fe and frequently came up to spend time on the ranch.

33 *Ibid.*

34 Frank Bond lecture at Los Alamos, 1991.

35 *Ibid*; Sharon Niederman, "Ranching Has Long History on the Valles Caldera," *Los Alamos Monitor*, February 16, 2003.

36 Interview with Mary Ann Bunten.

37 "Roundup Time in the Valle Grande," *Los Alamos Scientific Laboratory Community News*, October 20, 1960, pp. 6-7.

38 Bruce King, interview by the author, October 16, 2002.

39 Allen, 1989. The large body of work by Craig Allen and Thomas Swetnam details the fire ecology of the Jemez Mountains.

Chapter 7: Pat Dunigan and the Baca Land and Cattle Company

1 Hal K. Rothman, *On Rim and Ridges: The Los Alamos Area since 1880*, Lincoln: University of Nebraska Press, 1997, pp. 58-83; Thomas Altherr, "A National Park Second to None: Senator Clinton Anderson and the Valle Grande National Park Proposal, 1961-1966," unpublished manuscript, n.d., p. 3.

2 Rothman, 1997, pp. 161-162.

[3] Hal Rothman, *Bandelier National Monument: An Administrative History*, Santa Fe: Southwest Cultural Resources Center Professional Papers, No. 14, 1988, pp. 45-47.

[4] Mary D. Burchill, *Lady of the Canyon: Evelyn Cecil Frey*, Los Alamos: Otowi Crossing Press, 2001.

[5] Frank Bond, testimony before the Senate Subcommittee on Forest and Public Land Management, March 10, 2000.

[6] John V. Young, "Why Be Patient?" *Santa Fe New Mexican*, April 10, 1961; "Valle Grande Park Proposed," *Santa Fe New Mexican*, April 13, 1961.

[7] Altherr manuscript, p. 6; Richard Allen Baker, *Conservation Politics: The Senate Career of Clinton P. Anderson*, Albuquerque: University of New Mexico Press, 1985, pp. 167-169.

[8] Baker, 1985, pp. 167-169.

[9] Letter from Thomas Gallagher to Clinton Anderson, October 1961, as cited in Altherr manuscript, p. 8.

[10] Baker, pp. 169-170.

[11] Rothman, 1988, pp. 56-57.

[12] Joab Harrell, testimony before the Senate Committee on Energy and Natural Resources, March 10, 2000; Jim Conley, "Abilenian Taps Volcano for Energy," *Abilene Reporter News*, February 11, 1979.

[13] Jack Pearce, "Texans Buy 100,000 Acre Jemez Tract," *Santa Fe New Mexican*, January 30, 1963.

[14] "Texans Buy Baca Location," *The Atom*, February 14, 1963, pp. 6-7.

[15] Mark McMahon, "Construction Started, Race Track, Ski Resort Planned for Nearby Area," *Los Alamos Monitor*, April 25, 1963; "Baca Race Track Plans Confirmed," *Los Alamos Monitor*, May 2, 1963.

[16] Mark McMahon, "Dunigan Reveals Baca Site Plans," *Los Alamos Monitor*, May 23, 1963.

[17] "No Recreational Building in Baca," *Los Alamos Monitor*, June 27, 1963.

[18] Bill Huey, interview by the author, January 9, 2003.

[19] "Park Bill Passage Outlook Unknown," *Santa Fe New Mexican*, January 30, 1964; Rothman, 1988, pp. 58-59.

Chapter 8: High Grade to Low Grade: Logging the Caldera

[1] Deed of Trust between the Redondo Development Company and The Warren Savings Bank, April 1, 1915, Sandoval County, N.M. Records, New Mexico State Records Center and Archives, Santa Fe, New Mexico.

[2] Deed, Redondo Development to George Bond et al., April 8, 1926, Miscellaneous Record Book 2, Sandoval County Clerk's Office, p. 31.

[3] Vernon Glover, personal communication, December 11, 2002. Glover provided a copy of a 1988 memo from Thomas Gallagher, Jr. that discussed New Mexico Timber's operations on the Baca Location.

[4] Mary Ann Bond Bunten, interview by the author, November 20, 2002.

[5] Deed, Redondo Development to Robert Anderson Jr., July 19, 1935, Miscellaneous Record Book 4, Sandoval County Clerk's Office, p. 47.

[6] Vernon J. Glover, *Jemez Mountains Railroads*, Santa Fe: Historical Society of New Mexico, 1990, p. 36.

[7] Dan Scurlock, "Euro-American History of the Study Area," in *High Altitude Adaptations along Redondo Creek: The Baca Geothermal Anthropological Project*, Albuquerque: Office of Contract Archeology, University of New Mexico, 1981, p. 144.

[8] "Land Classification Map, Baca Location No. 1," prepared for the Baca Land and Cattle Company by Frank and Dean Solinsky, Inc., 1963. Additional information on this early logging period comes from the first sequence of aerial photographs taken of the Jemez Mountain in 1935. Discussions with landscape ecologist Craig Allen in May 2002 provided additional information. The story can still be read in the landscape itself.

[9] Glover, p. 36.

[10] Santa Fe National Forest, New Mexico, *Report on the Study of the Baca Location No. 1*, 1993, pp. 21-23.

[11] "Park, Forest Services Agree on Jemez Crater Plan," *Los Alamos Scientific Laboratory Community News*, December 14, 1962, p. 2.

[12] "Cutting May Mar Baca Location," *Los Alamos Scientific Laboratory Community News*, February 1, 1963, p. 4.

[13] Andrew Dunigan, interview by the author, November 27, 2002. Barbara Johnson of the Quivira Coalition, which sponsors an annual award in Burch's honor, provided additional information on Clarence Burch.

[14] "Baca Location to Change," *Los Alamos Monitor*, December 17, 1970.

[15] "Logging Threatens Scenic Valle Grande," *Los Alamos Monitor*, November 26, 1970.

[16] "Timber Co. Pays $202,278 Damages," *Los Alamos Monitor*, June 9, 1971.

[17] "Baca Location Timber Is Sold to Ranch Owner," *Santa Fe New Mexican*, June 30, 1972.

Chapter 9: Steam, Cows, Elk, and Hollywood

[1] Jamie Gardner, interview by the author, March 1, 2002.

[2] "Geothermal Adventures in the Jemez," *Los Alamos Monitor*, November 26, 1974.

[3] "Steam Well Drilled on Baca Location," *Los Alamos Monitor*, October 22, 1970; Jim Conley, "Abilenian Taps Volcano for Energy," *Abilene Reporter News*, February 11, 1979.

[4] "Union Oil Co. Signs Baca Steam Agreement," *Los Alamos Monitor*, June 10, 1971; Van Court and Company, *Real Estate Appraisal, Baca Location No. 1*, 1998, p. 17.

[5] Conley, 1979.

[6] Gregory Nibert, testimony before the Senate Subcommittee on Forest and Public Land Management, March 10, 2000.

[7] "Snag Shouldn't Halt Baca Project," *Los Alamos Monitor*, February 28, 1980.

[8] Terry England, "Geothermal Project Impact is Documented," *Los Alamos Monitor*, January 29, 1980.

[9] Terry England, "DOE Delays Final Decision on Baca Geothermal Power Plant," *Los Alamos Monitor*, February 26, 1980.

[10] Terry England, "Indians Consider Lawsuit to Halt Geothermal Plant," *Los Alamos Monitor*, March 7, 1980.

[11] Terry England, "Baca Opponent Happy but Wary About Shutdown," *Los Alamos Monitor*, January 24, 1982. Subsequent research by Fraser Goff and Lisa Shevenell demonstrated that the hot springs in the Cañon de San Diego were indeed fed by waters from the Valles Caldera hydrothermal reservoir.

[12] Jane Seagrave, "Future of Jemez Hinges on Power Plant Debate," *Los Alamos Monitor*, November 30, 1980.

[13] "Elusive Hot Water Forces Baca Abandonment," *Los Alamos Monitor*, January 22, 1982.

[14] Nibert testimony, 2000; Joab Harrell, testimony before the Senate Committee on Energy and Natural Resources, March 10, 2000.

[15] Interview with Jamie Gardner.

[16] F. Goff, J. Rowley, J. N. Gardner, W. Hawkins, S. Goff, R. Charles, D. Wachs, L. Maassen, and G. Heiken, "Initial results from VC-1, first Continental Scientific Drilling Program core hole in Valles Caldera, New Mexico," *Journal of Geophysical Research*, vol. 91, 1986, pp. 1742-1752.

[17] Interview with Jamie Gardner.

[18] Fraser Goff and Cathy J. Janik. "Reservoir Geochemistry from Flow Tests of Scientific Corehole, Sulphur Springs, Valles Caldera." In *New Mexico Geological Society Guidebook, Geology of the Jemez Mountains*, Socorro: New Mexico Geological Society, 1996, p. 52.

[19] Interview with Jamie Gardner.

[20] Palemon Martinez, personal communication, March 5, 2002.

[21] Bill Huey, interview by the author, January 9, 2003.

[22] Van Court and Company, 1998, p. 29.

[23] Craig Allen, "Report to the Baca Land and Cattle Company," 1997, unpublished report in the Valles Caldera National Preserve files.

[24] *Ibid*. With new fall and winter habitat in the Cerro Grande burn area on the east side of the Sierra de los Valles, the elk population will undoubtedly continue to grow.

[25] Deanna Morgan Kirby, *Just Crazy to Ski: A Fifty-Year History of Skiing at Los Alamos*, Los Alamos: Los Alamos Historical Society, in press, 2003.

[26] Harrell, testimony, 2000; Rothman, 1988, p. 60. The stipulation for a fence seemed a reasonable caveat, but the Park Service never came up with the necessary funding. In 1987, David Donohue with the Park Service said another 18 miles of fence were needed with an estimated cost of $251,000. The fence has yet to be completed.

[27] *Movies Made in New Mexico: 1898-1999*, edited by John Raymond Armijo, Santa Fe: New Mexico Film Office, 1999; author interview with Andrew Dunigan, November 27, 2002.

Chapter 10: The Road to Preservation

[1] Van Court and Company, *Real Estate Appraisal, Baca Location No. 1*, 1998, p. 24.

[2] Hal Rothman, *Bandelier National Monument: An Administrative History*, Santa Fe: Southwest Cultural Resources Center Professional Papers, No. 14, 1988, p. 61.

[3] National Park Service. *Valles Caldera: Study of Alternatives*, Washington: U.S. Department of the Interior, 1979.

[4] Bill Huey, interview by the author, January 9, 2003; Joab Harrell, testimony before the Senate Committee on Energy and Natural Resources, March 10, 2000.

[5] Hal Rothman, *On Rims and Ridges: The Los Alamos Area Since 1880*, Lincoln: University of Nebraska Press, 1992, pp. 299-300.

[6] Sandi Doughton-Evans, "National Park Proposed in Jemez," *Los Alamos Monitor*, February 5, 1987.

[7] Sandi Doughton-Evans, "Jemez Park Opposed," *Los Alamos Monitor*, March 3, 1987.

[8] Sandi Doughton-Evans, "Jemez National Park Proposal Withdrawn," *Los Alamos Monitor*, March 13, 1987.

[9] "Baca Owners Don't Want to Sell," *Los Alamos Monitor*, April 1, 1987.

[10] Santa Fe National Forest, *Report on the Study of the Baca Location No. 1*, 1993, pp. 2, 49-50.

[11] Gary Ziehe, interview by the author, November 6, 2002. Ziehe was on Domenici's staff during the time of the negotiations and drafted much of the Valles Caldera preservation legislation.

[12] Karen McPherson, "U.S. May Buy Valle Grande Land," *Albuquerque Tribune*, September 24, 1997.

[13] John Hill, "Feds Tour Majestic Valle Grande, Which a N.M. Senator Proposes They Buy, Maintain," *Albuquerque Tribune*, October 17, 1997.

[14] Martin Frentzel, "Buying Back the Baca," *Trout*, Autumn 1998, pp. 18-23.

[15] Ian Hoffman, "GOP Blocks Purchase of Baca Ranch," *Albuquerque Journal*, June 20, 1998; Michael Coleman, "Redmond Changes Stance on Baca Ranch," *Albuquerque Journal*, July 25, 1998.

[16] Coleman, 1998.

[17] Patrick Armijo, "Redmond: Use Arts Fund to Buy Ranch," *Albuquerque Journal*, July 23, 1998; Michael Coleman, "Redmond Changes Stance on Baca Ranch," *Albuquerque Journal*, July 25, 1998.

[18] Interview with Gary Ziehe.

[19] The Presidio Trust Act, H.R. 4236, P.L. 104-333, November 12, 1996.

[20] Interview with Gary Ziehe; Ian Hoffman, "Domenici Lassos Way to Buy Baca Ranch," *Albuquerque Journal North*, July 31, 1999.

[21] Interview with Gary Ziehe.

[22] Shonda Novak, "Boosters Cling to Faint Hopes for Baca Ranch," *Albuquerque Tribune*, January 8, 1999; Associated Press, "Feds Have Made No Effort to Restart Talks on Baca Ranch, Owners Say," January 27, 1999.

[23] Associated Press, "Texas Family May Again Seek Sale of Vast New Mexico Ranch," July 17, 1999; interview with Bill Huey.

[24] Jessica Wehrman, "Baca Ranch Sale Gains New Life," *Albuquerque Tribune*, September 9, 1999.

[25] Associated Press, "Texas Family May Again Seek Sale of Vast New Mexico Ranch," July 17, 1999; Jessica Wehrman, "Baca Ranch Worth Its Price," *Albuquerque Tribune*, March 11, 2000.

[26] Tim Archuleta, "Congress Approves Baca Ranch Purchase," *Albuquerque Tribune*, July 12, 2000.

[27] Congressional Record of the 106th Congress. Public Law 106-248, Valles Caldera Preservation Act.

[28] David Simon, testimony before the Senate Committee on Energy and Natural Resources, March 10, 2000.

[29] Exceptions can occur, however: "Nothing in this subsection shall preclude—(A) the use and maintenance of roads and trails existing as of the date of enactment of this Act; (B) the construction, use and maintenance of new trails, and the relocation of existing roads, if located to avoid Native American religious and cultural sites; and (C) motorized access necessary to administer the area by the Trust (including measures required in emergencies involving the health or safety of persons within the area)."

[30] The law also provided for the Secretary of Agriculture to keep the property closed to all recreational use for as long as necessary to develop a management plan. Public access to the Preserve was limited until June 2003.

Chapter 11: Balancing Act: Working Ranch, Public Playground, and Natural Preserve

[1] Minutes of the Valles Caldera Trust Listening Session, March 9, 2000.

[2] Minutes of the Valles Caldera Trust, December 13, 2001.

[3] The author was present for the release of the first cattle on the Preserve, and was the guide for the first hiking tour.

INDEX